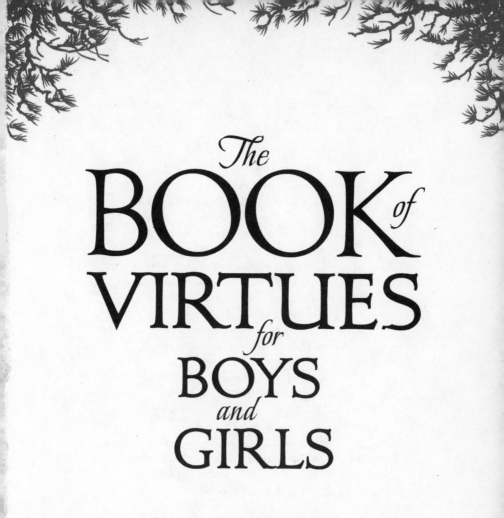

The BOOK of VIRTUES for BOYS and GIRLS

EDITED WITH COMMENTARY
AND AFTERWORD BY

William J. Bennett

INTRODUCTION BY Doug Flutie

Aladdin
NEW YORK LONDON TORONTO SYDNEY

ALADDIN

An imprint of Simon & Schuster Children's Publishing Division

1230 Avenue of the Americas, New York, NY 10020

Copyright © 1997, 2008 by William J. Bennett

Introduction copyright © 2008 by Doug Flutie

An earlier edition of this work was published in 1997 by Simon & Schuster

Books for Young Readers as *The Book of Virtues for Young People*.

Designed by Mike Rosamilia

The text of this book was set in Perpetua.

Manufactured in the United States of America

First Aladdin Paperbacks edition September 2008

2 4 6 8 10 9 7 5 3 1

Library of Congress Cataloging-in-Publication Data

The book of virtues for boys and girls : a treasury of great moral stories /

[compiled] by William J. Bennett ; introduction by Doug Flutie.—

1st Aladdin Paperbacks ed.

p. cm.

Abridged ed. of: The book of virtues for young people. 1996.

ISBN-13: 978-1-4169-7125-2

ISBN-10: 1-4169-7125-4

1. Literature—Collections. 2. Conduct of life—Literary collections.

I. Bennett, William J. (William John), 1943–

II. Book of virtues for young people.

PN6014.B695 2008

808.7—dc22

2008017077

Table of Contents

Introduction

Using quotes, narratives, and poetry, Dr. Bennett illustrates some important qualities: friendship, work, courage, honesty, and loyalty. He discusses why each is a virtue, and how to attain these virtues in life. Dr. Bennett shows us why a virtuous lifestyle is important—to the person and their community.

Like Dr. Bennett, I believe friendship is about loyalty and trust. Looking over my shoulder and knowing that I was not alone on the field gave me the sense of stability I needed to excel. Many of my teammates became real friends. These friends were there for me when I went through tough times on the field and off.

Hard work can offer real rewards. While most people think of football as a fantasy job, they don't see the behind-the-scenes time and effort professional athletes put into practice. I was not the best or tallest athlete, but I was able to compensate by working harder. I watched game film, rarely took a day off, and listened to the advice my coaches offered me. And my efforts paid off.

To me, courage is the ability to muster up the mental strength to confront one's fears. The greatest battle of my life came when my son, Doug Jr., was diagnosed with autism. Helping to care for him as he lived with autism and speaking out about it to generate awareness for the disease has been one of the toughest and most rewarding things I have done. My wife and I have had the pleasure of helping thousands of families through the Doug Flutie, Jr. Foundation for Autism.

Honesty is one of the most important characteristics of all. There are many kinds of people, and you may be hurt when you come across someone dishonest. But it's important to keep looking for the people you can trust.

Loyalty has had amazing, positive effects on my life. The loyalty I have received from my wife, teammates, brothers, and fans has helped me over the past three decades. I try to be loyal to those who have been there for me as well. Life wouldn't mean much if we had no one to rely on for support, and if we were not there for others.

My experiences playing football and living a full life have made me appreciate the importance of having integrity. Just as with any skill, living a virtuous lifestyle takes practice. In this book, Dr. Bennett discusses the vital role that virtues and morals play in such a lifestyle in a way that young readers can appreciate. I hope they enjoy it as much as I did.

—Doug Flutie

FRIENDSHIP

Friendship

Why do we want friends? The obvious answer is that friends make us happy. They make life more interesting and fun for us. They share our tastes, our desires, our sense of humor.

But real friendship is based on more than just hanging around with each other and joking with each other. The ancient Greek philosopher Aristotle put it this way: "We may describe friendly feeling toward any one as wishing for him what you believe to be good things, not for your own sake but for his, and being inclined, so far as you can, to bring these things about."

In other words, real friends give each other virtues, or "good things," as Aristotle put it. Friends give loyalty to one another, as in the story of Jonathan and David in this chapter. They give trust as in the story of Damon and Pythias. They give help in times of need, as in the story of Ruth and Naomi.

Friends naturally try to make each other better people. They try to lift each other. They help each other make the right decisions and aim for worthy goals. Being a friend does not always require doing what your friend wants you to do. Rather, it requires doing what you believe is best for your friend.

All of this means you must choose your friends wisely. Your friends tell you a lot about yourself. They tell you what kind of person you may turn out to be. Good friends help lift you up, but bad friends will drag you down. If they have bad habits, there's a good chance you'll end up with those bad habits, too. So if you can't persuade them to change their ways, you'll do better to find some new friends.

Of course, for many people, finding and making new friends is a tough process. But it doesn't have to be so hard if you think less about *having* friends and more about *being* a friend. You'll make many more friends by being interested in people than you will by trying to get people interested in you. And by being genuinely interested in other people, you'll discover that friendship does not just bring you happiness. It will *improve* your happiness by making you a better person.

A Time to Talk

ROBERT FROST

Work always calls us. But we make time for friends when they call, too.

> When a friend calls to me from the road
> And slows his horse to a meaning walk,
> I don't stand still and look around
> On all the hills I haven't hoed,
> And shout from where I am, What is it?
> No, not as there is a time to talk.
> I thrust my hoe in the mellow ground,
> Blade-end up and five feet tall,
> And plod: I go up to the stone wall
> For a friendly visit.

Childhood and Poetry

PABLO NERUDA

This story by Chilean poet Pablo Neruda (1904-1973) suggests that every time we offer friendship to someone we do not know, we strengthen our bond with all humanity.

One time, investigating in the backyard of our house in Temuco the tiny objects and miniscule beings of my world, I came upon a hole in one of the boards of the fence. I looked through the hole and saw a landscape like that behind our house, uncared for and wild. I moved back a few steps, because I sensed vaguely that something was about to happen. All of a sudden a hand appeared—a tiny hand of a boy about my own age. By the time I came close again, the hand was gone, and in its place there was a marvelous white sheep.

The sheep's wool was faded. Its wheels had escaped. All of this only made it more authentic. I had never seen such a wonderful sheep. I looked back through the hole but the boy had disappeared. I went into the house and brought out a treasure of my own: a pine cone, opened, full of odor and resin, which I adored. I set it down in the same spot and went off with the sheep.

I never saw either the hand or the boy again. And I have never again seen a sheep like that either. The toy I lost finally in a fire. But even now, in 1954, almost fifty years old, whenever I pass a toy shop, I look furtively into the window, but it's no use. They don't make sheep like that anymore.

I have been a lucky man. To feel the intimacy of brothers is a marvelous thing in life. To feel the love of people whom we love is a fire that feeds our life. But to feel the affection that comes from those whom we do not know, from those unknown to us, who are watching over our sleep and solitude, over our dangers and our weaknesses— that is something still greater and more beautiful because it widens out the boundaries of our being, and unites all living things.

That exchange brought home to me for the first time a precious idea: that all of humanity is somehow together. That experience came to me again much later; this time it stood out strikingly against a background of trouble and persecution.

It won't surprise you then that I attempted to give something resiny, earthlike and fragrant in exchange for human brotherhood. Just as I once left the pine cone by the fence, I have since left my words on the door of so many people who were unknown to me, people in prison, or hunted, or alone.

That is the great lesson I learned in my childhood, in the backyard of a lonely house. Maybe it was nothing but a game two boys played who didn't know each other and wanted to pass to the other some good things of life. Yet maybe this small and mysterious exchange of gifts remained inside me also, deep and indestructible, giving my poetry light.

Damon and Pythias

This story takes place in Syracuse in the fourth century B.C. Even today, the tale of Damon and Pythias sets the standard for the deepest friendships, which give every reason for confidence and leave no room for doubts.

Damon and Pythias had been the best of friends since childhood. Each trusted the other like a brother, and each knew in his heart there was nothing he would not do for his friend. Eventually the time came for them to prove the depth of their devotion. It happened this way.

Dionysius, the ruler of Syracuse, grew annoyed when he heard about the speeches Pythias was giving. The young scholar was telling the public that no man should have unlimited power over another, and that absolute tyrants were unjust kings. In a fit of rage, Dionysius summoned Pythias and his friend.

"Who do you think you are, spreading unrest among the people?" he demanded.

"I spread only the truth," Pythias answered. "There can be nothing wrong with that."

"And does your truth hold that kings have too much power and that their laws are not good for their subjects?"

"If a king has seized power without permission of the people, then that is what I say."

"This kind of talk is treason," Dionysius shouted. "You are conspiring to overthrow me. Retract what you've said, or face the consequences."

"I will retract nothing," Pythias answered.

"Then you will die. Do you have any last requests?"

"Yes. Let me go home just long enough to say goodbye to my wife and children and to put my household in order."

"I see you not only think I'm unjust, you think I'm stupid as well," Dionysius laughed scornfully. "If I let you leave Syracuse, I have no doubt I will never see you again."

"I will give you a pledge," Pythias said.

"What kind of pledge could you possibly give to make

me think you will ever return?" Dionysius demanded.

At that instant Damon, who had stood quietly beside his friend, stepped forward.

"I will be his pledge," he said. "Keep me here in Syracuse, as your prisoner, until Pythias returns. Our friendship is well known to you. You can be sure Pythias will return so long as you hold me."

Dionysius studied the two friends silently. "Very well," he said at last. "But if you are willing to take the place of your friend, you must be willing to accept his sentence if he breaks his promise. If Pythias does not return to Syracuse, you will die in his place."

"He will keep his word," Damon replied. "I have no doubt of that."

Pythias was allowed to go free for a time, and Damon was thrown into prison. After several days, when Pythias failed to reappear, Dionysius's curiosity got the better of him, and he went to the prison to see if Damon was yet sorry he had made such a bargain.

"Your time is almost up," the ruler of Syracuse sneered. "It will be useless to beg for mercy. You were a fool to rely on your friend's promise. Did you really think he would sacrifice his life for you or anyone else?"

"He has merely been delayed," Damon answered steadily. "The winds have kept him from sailing, or perhaps he has met with some accident on the road. But if it is humanly possible, he will be here on time. I am as confident of his virtue as I am of my own existence."

Dionysius was startled at the prisoner's confidence. "We shall soon see," he said, and left Damon in his cell.

The fatal day arrived. Damon was brought from prison and led before the executioner. Dionysius greeted him with a smug smile.

"It seems your friend has not turned up," he laughed. "What do you think of him now?"

"He is my friend," Damon answered. "I trust him."

Even as he spoke, the doors flew open and Pythias staggered into the room. He was pale and bruised and half speechless from exhaustion. He rushed to the arms of his friend.

"You are safe, praise the gods," he gasped. "It seemed as though the fates were conspiring against us. My ship was wrecked in a storm, and then bandits attacked me on the road. But I refused to give up hope, and at last I've made it back in time. I am ready to receive my sentence of death."

Dionysius heard his words with astonishment. His eyes and his heart were opened. It was impossible for him to resist the power of such constancy.

"The sentence is revoked," he declared. "I never believed that such faith and loyalty could exist in friendship. You have shown me how wrong I was, and it is only right that you be rewarded with your freedom. But I ask that in return you do me one great service."

"What service do you mean?" the friends asked.

"Teach me how to be part of so worthy a friendship."

Helen Keller and Anne Sullivan

There is no friendship more sacred than that between student and teacher, and one of the greatest of these was the friend-

ship of Helen Keller (1880-1968) and Anne Mansfield Sullivan (1866-1936).

Illness destroyed Helen Keller's sight and hearing when she was not two years old, leaving her cut off from the world. For nearly five years she grew up, as she later described it, "wild and unruly, giggling and chuckling to express pleasure; kicking, scratching, uttering the choked screams of the deaf-mute to indicate the opposite."

Anne Sullivan's arrival at the Kellers' Alabama home from the Perkins Institution for the Blind in Boston changed Helen's life. Sullivan herself had been half-blind from an eye infection from which she never fully recovered, and she came to Helen with experience, unbending dedication, and love. Through the sense of touch she was able to make contact with the young girl's mind, and within three years she had taught Helen to read and write in Braille. By sixteen, Helen could speak well enough to go to preparatory school and college. She graduated cum laude from Radcliffe in 1904, and devoted the rest of her life to helping the blind and deaf-blind, as her teacher had done. The two women continued their remarkable friendship until Anne's death.

Helen wrote about Anne Sullivan's arrival in her autobiography, The Story of My Life.

The most important day I remember in all my life is the one on which my teacher, Anne Mansfield Sullivan, came to me. I am filled with wonder when I consider the immeasurable contrasts between the two lives which it connects. It was the third of March, 1887, three months before I was seven years old.

On that afternoon of the eventful day, I stood on the porch, dumb, expectant. I guessed vaguely from my mother's signs and from the hurrying to and fro in the house that something unusual was about to happen, so I went to the door and waited on the steps. The afternoon sun penetrated the mass of honeysuckle that covered the porch, and fell on my upturned face. My fingers lingered almost unconsciously on the familiar leaves and blossoms which had just come forth to greet the sweet Southern spring. I did not know what the future held of marvel or surprise for me. Anger and bitterness had preyed upon me continually for weeks and a deep languor had succeeded this passionate struggle.

Have you ever been at sea in a dense fog, when it seemed as if a tangible white darkness shut you in, and the great ship, tense and anxious, groped her way toward the shore with plummet and sounding-line, and you waited with beating heart for something to happen? I was like that ship before my education began, only I was without compass or sounding-line, and had no way of knowing how near the harbor was. "Light! give me light!" was the wordless cry of my soul, and the light of love shone on me in that very hour.

I felt approaching footsteps. I stretched out my hand as I supposed to my mother. Someone took it, and I was caught up and held close in the arms of her who had come to reveal all things to me and, more than all things else, to love me.

The morning after my teacher came she led me into her room and gave me a doll. The little blind children at the Perkins

Institution had sent it and Laura Bridgman had dressed it; but I did not know this until afterward. When I had played with it a little while, Miss Sullivan slowly spelled into my hand the word "d-o-l-l." I was at once interested in this finger play and tried to imitate it. When I finally succeeded in making the letters correctly I was flushed with childish pleasure and pride. Running downstairs to my mother I held up my hand and made the letters for *doll*. I did not know that I was spelling a word or even that words existed; I was simply making my fingers go in monkey-like imitation. In the days that followed I learned to spell in this uncomprehending way a great many words, among them, *pin, hat, cup* and a few verbs like *sit, stand,* and *walk*. But my teacher had been with me several weeks before I understood that everything has a name.

One day, while I was playing with my new doll, Miss Sullivan put my big rag doll into my lap also, spelled "d-o-l-l" and tried to make me understand that "d-o-l-l" applied to both. Earlier in the day we had had a tussle over the words "m-u-g" and "w-a-t-e-r." Miss Sullivan had tried to impress upon me that "m-u-g" is *mug* and that "w-a-t-e-r" is *water,* but I persisted in confounding the two. In despair she had dropped the subject for the time, only to renew it at the first opportunity. I became impatient at her repeated attempts and, seizing the new doll, I dashed it upon the floor. I was keenly delighted when I felt the fragments of the broken doll at my feet. Neither sorrow nor regret followed my passionate outburst. I had not loved the doll. In the still, dark world in which I lived, there was no strong sentiment or tenderness. I felt my teacher sweep the fragments to one side of the hearth, and

I had a sense of satisfaction that the cause of my discomfort was removed. She brought me my hat, and I knew I was going out into the warm sunshine. This thought, if a wordless sensation may be called a thought, made me hop and skip with pleasure.

We walked down the path to the well-house, attracted by the fragrance of the honeysuckle with which it was covered. Someone was drawing water and my teacher placed my hand under the spout. As the cool stream gushed over one hand she spelled into the other the word *water*, first slowly, then rapidly. I stood still, my whole attention fixed upon the motions of her fingers. Suddenly I felt a misty consciousness as of something forgotten—a thrill of returning thought; and somehow the mystery of language was revealed to me. I knew then that "w-a-t-e-r" meant the wonderful cool something that was flowing over my hand. That living word awakened my soul, gave it light, hope, joy, set it free! There were barriers still, it is true, but barriers that could in time be swept away.

I left the well-house eager to learn. Everything had a name, and each name gave birth to a new thought. As we returned to the house every object which I touched seemed to quiver with life. That was because I saw everything with the strange, new sight that had come to me. On entering the door I remembered the doll I had broken. I felt my way to the hearth and picked up the pieces. I tried vainly to put them together. Then my eyes filled with tears; for I realized what I had done, and for the first time I felt repentance and sorrow.

I learned a great many new words that day. I do not remember what they all were; but I do know that *mother, father, sister, teacher* were among them—words that were to make the world blossom for me, "like Aaron's rod, with flowers." It would have been difficult to find a happier child than I was as I lay in my crib at the close of that eventful day and lived over the joys it had brought me, and for the first time longed for a new day to come.

Anne Sullivan, in her letters, described the "miracle" she saw taking place in Helen.

March 20, 1887

My heart is singing for joy this morning. A miracle has happened! The light of understanding has shone upon my little pupil's mind, and behold, all things are changed!

The wild little creature of two weeks ago has been transformed into a gentle child. She is sitting by me as I write, her face serene and happy, crocheting a long red chain of Scotch wool. She learned the stitch this week, and is very proud of the achievement. When she succeeded in making a chain that would reach across the room, she patted herself on the arm and put the first work of her hands lovingly against her cheek. She lets me kiss her now, and when she is in a particularly gentle mood, she will sit in my lap for a minute or two; but she does not return my caresses. The great step—the step that counts—has been taken. The little savage has learned her first lesson in obedience, and finds the yoke easy. It now remains my pleasant task to direct and mold the beautiful intelligence that is beginning to stir in the child-soul. Already people remark the change in Helen. Her father looks in at us morning and evening as he goes to and from his office, and sees her contentedly stringing her beads or making horizontal lines on her sewing card, and exclaims, "How quiet she is!" When I came, her movements were so insistent that one always felt there was something unnatural and almost weird about her. I have noticed also that she eats much less, a fact which troubles her father so much that he is anxious to get her home. He says she is homesick. I don't agree with him; but I suppose we shall have to leave our little bower very soon.

Helen has learned several nouns this week. "M-u-g" and "m-i-l-k," have given her more trouble than other words. When she spells *milk,* she points to the mug, and when she spells *mug,* she makes the sign for pouring or drinking, which shows that she has confused the words. She has no idea yet that everything has a name.

April 5, 1887

I must write you a line this morning because something very important has happened. Helen has taken the second great step in her education. She has learned that *everything has a name, and that the manual alphabet is the key to everything she wants to know.*

In a previous letter I think I wrote you that "mug" and "milk" had given Helen more trouble than all the rest. She confused the nouns with the verb "drink." She didn't know the word for "drink," but went through the pantomime of drinking whenever she spelled "mug" or "milk." This morning, while she was washing, she wanted to know the name for "water." When she wants to know the name of anything, she points to it and pats my hand.

I spelled "w-a-t-e-r" and thought no more about it until after breakfast. Then it occurred to me that with the help of this new word I might succeed in straightening out the "mug-milk" difficulty. We went out to the pump-house, and I made Helen hold her mug under the spout while I pumped. As the cold water gushed forth, filling the mug, I spelled "w-a-t-e-r" in Helen's free hand. The word coming so close upon the sensation of cold water rushing over her hand seemed to startle her. She dropped the mug and stood as one transfixed. A new light came into her face. She spelled "water" several times. Then she dropped on the ground and asked for its name and pointed to the pump and the trellis, and suddenly turning round she asked for my name. I spelled "Teacher." Just then the nurse brought Helen's little sister into the pump-house, and Helen spelled "baby" and pointed to the nurse. All the way back to the house she was highly excited, and learned the name of every object she touched, so that in a few hours she had thirty new words to her vocabulary. Here are some of them: *Door, open, shut, give, go, come,* and a great many more.

P.S.—I didn't finish my letter in time to get it posted last night; so I shall add a line. Helen got up this morning like a radiant fairy. She has flitted from object to object, asking the name of everything and kissing me for very gladness. Last night when I got in bed, she stole into my arms of her own accord and kissed me for the first time, and I thought my heart would burst, so full was it of joy.

Jonathan and David

RETOLD BY JESSE LYMAN HURLBUT

Sometimes the duties of friendship compete with other obligations and affections. The story of Jonathan, told in the first book of Samuel in the Bible, is one such instance. Jonathan was the eldest son and heir of King Saul of Israel. He was also David's sworn friend. After David killed Goliath, Saul grew jealous of his popularity, and fearing that he would eventually become king, sought to murder him. Jonathan's defense of David, made doubly painful because of his duties to his father and his own claim to the throne, is one of our greatest examples of loyalty and friendship.

After David had slain the giant he was brought before King Saul, still holding the giant's head. Saul did not remember in this bold fighting man the boy who a few years before had played in his presence. He took him into his own house and made him an officer among his soldiers. David was as wise and as brave in the army as he had been when facing the giant, and very soon he was in command of a thousand men. All the men loved him, both in Saul's court and in his camp, for David had the spirit that drew all hearts toward him.

When David was returning from his battle with the Philistines, the women of Israel came to meet him out of the cities, with instruments of music, singing and dancing, and they sang:

"Saul has slain his thousands,
And David his ten thousands."

This made Saul very angry, for he was jealous and suspicious in his spirit. He thought constantly of Samuel's words, that God would take the kingdom from him and would give it to one who was more worthy of it. He began to think that perhaps this young man, who had come in a single day to greatness before the people, might try to make himself king.

His former feeling of unhappiness again came over Saul. He raved in his house, talking as a man talks who is crazed. By this time they all knew that David was a musician, and they called him again to play on his harp and to sing before the troubled king. But now, in his madness, Saul would not listen to David's voice. Twice he threw his spear at him; but each time David leaped aside, and the spear went into the wall of the house.

Saul was afraid of David, for he saw that the Lord was with David, as the Lord was no longer with himself. He would have killed David, but did not dare kill him, because everybody loved David. Saul said to himself, "Though I cannot kill him myself, I will have him killed by the Philistines."

And he sent David out on dangerous errands of war; but David came home in safety, all the greater and the more beloved after each victory. Saul said, "I will give you my daughter Merab for your wife if you will fight the Philistines for me."

David fought the Philistines; but when he came home from the war he found that Merab, who had been promised to him, had been given as wife to another man. Saul had another daughter, named Michal. She loved David, and showed her love for him. Then Saul sent word to David, saying, "You shall have Michal, my daughter, for your wife when you have killed a hundred Philistines."

Then David went out and fought the Philistines, and killed two hundred of them; and they brought the word to Saul. Then Saul gave him his daughter Michal as his wife; but he was all the more afraid of David as he saw him growing in power and drawing nearer the throne of the kingdom.

But if Saul hated David, Saul's son Jonathan saw David's courage, and the soul of Jonathan was knit to the soul of David, and Jonathan loved him as his own soul. He took off his own royal robe and his sword and his bow, and gave them all to David. It grieved Jonathan greatly that his father, Saul, was so jealous of David. He spoke to his father and said: "Let not the king do harm to David; for David has been faithful to the king, and he has done great things for the kingdom. He took his life in his hand, and killed the Philistines, and won a great victory for the Lord and for the people. Why should you seek to kill an innocent man?"

For the time Saul listened to Jonathan, and said, "As the Lord lives, David shall not be put to death."

And again David sat at the king's table, among the princes; and when Saul was troubled again David played on his harp and sang before him. But once more Saul's jealous anger arose, and he threw his spear at David. David was watchful and quick. He leaped aside and, as before, the spear fastened into the wall.

Saul sent men to David's house to seize him; but Michal, Saul's daughter, who was David's wife, let David down out of the window, so that he escaped. She placed an image on David's bed and covered it with the bedclothes. When the men came, she said, "David is ill in the bed and cannot go."

They brought the word to Saul, and he said, "Bring him to me in the bed, just as he is."

When the image was found in David's bed, David was in a safe place, far away. David went to Samuel at Ramah, and stayed with him among the men who were prophets worshipping God and singing and speaking God's word. Saul heard that David was there and sent men to take him. But when these men came and saw Samuel and the prophets praising God and praying, the same spirit came on them, and they began to praise and to pray. Saul sent other men, but these also, when they came among the prophets, felt the same power and joined in the worship.

Finally, Saul said, "If no other man will bring David to me, I will go myself and take him."

And Saul went to Ramah; but when he came near to the company of the worshippers, praising God, and praying, and preaching, the same spirit came on Saul. He, too, began to join in the songs and the prayers, and stayed there all that day and that night, worshipping God very earnestly. When the next day he went again to his home in Gibeah, his feeling was changed for the time, and he was again friendly to David.

But David knew that Saul was at heart his bitter enemy and would kill him if he could as soon as his madness came upon him.

He met Jonathan out in the field away from the palace. Jonathan said to David:

"Stay away from the king's table for a few days, and I will find out how he feels toward you, and will tell you. Perhaps even now my father may become your friend. But if he is to be your enemy, I know that the Lord is with you and that Saul will not succeed against you. Promise me that as long as you live you will be kind to me, and not only to me while I live, but to my children after me."

Jonathan believed, as many others believed, that David would yet become the king of Israel, and he was willing to give up to David his right to be king, such was his great love for him. That day a promise was made between Jonathan and David, that they and their children and those who should come after them, should be friends forever.

Jonathan said to David, "I will find how my father feels toward you and will bring you word. After three days I will be here with my bow and arrows, and I will send a little boy out near your place of hiding, and I will shoot three arrows. If I say to the boy, 'Run, find the arrows, they are on this side of you,' then you can come safely, for the king will not harm you. But if I call out to the boy, 'The arrows are away beyond you,' that will mean that there is danger, and you must hide from the king."

So David stayed away from Saul's table for two days. At first Saul said nothing of his absence, but at last he said:

"Why has not the son of Jesse come to meals yesterday and today?"

And Jonathan said, "David asked leave of me to go to his

home at Bethlehem and visit his oldest brother."

Then Saul was very angry. He cried out, "You are a disobedient son! Why have you chosen this enemy of mine as your best friend? Do you not know that as long as he is alive you can never be king? Send after him, and let him be brought to me, for he shall surely die!"

Saul was so fierce in his anger that he threw his spear at his own son Jonathan. Jonathan rose up from the table, so anxious for his friend David that he could eat nothing. The next day, at the hour agreed upon, Jonathan went out into the field with a little boy. He said to the boy, "Run out yonder, and be ready to find the arrows that I shoot."

And as the boy was running Jonathan shot arrows beyond him, and he called out, "The arrows are away beyond you; run quickly and find them."

The boy ran and found the arrows, and brought them to Jonathan. He gave the bow and arrows to the boy, saying to him, "Take them back to the city. I will stay here awhile."

And as soon as the boy was out of sight David came from his hiding place and ran to Jonathan. They fell into each other's arms and kissed each other again and again, and wept together. For David knew now that he must no longer hope to be safe in Saul's hands. He must leave home, wife, friends, and his father's house, and hide wherever he could from the hate of King Saul.

Jonathan said to him, "Go in peace; for we have sworn together saying, 'The Lord shall be between you and me and between your children and my children forever.'"

Then Jonathan went again to his father's palace, and David went out to find a hiding place.

Ruth and Naomi
RETOLD BY JESSE LYMAN HURLBUT

The book of Ruth in the Bible is the story of a widow's courageous decision to leave Moab, her homeland, and travel to Judah with her Hebrew mother-in-law, who has lost her own husband and sons. Ruth's words to Naomi are one of the greatest statements of friendship and loyalty in all of literature: "Whither thou goest, I will go; and where thou lodgest, I will lodge: thy people shall be my people, and thy God my God. Where thou diest, will I die, and there will I be buried." In Judah, Ruth's fidelity and kindness were rewarded with the love of Boaz, and through marriage to him she became the great-grandmother of King David.

In the time of the judges in Israel, a man named Elimelech was living in the town of Bethlehem, in the tribe of Judah, about six miles south of Jerusalem. His wife's name was Naomi, and his two sons were Mahlon and Chilion. For some years the crops were poor, and food was scarce in Judah; and Elimelech, with his family, went to live in the land of Moab, which was on the east of the Dead Sea, as Judah was on the west.

There they stayed ten years, and in that time Elimelech died. His two sons married women of the country of Moab, one woman name Orpah, the other named Ruth. But the two young men also died in the land of Moab, so that Naomi and her two daughters-in-law were all left widows.

Naomi heard that God had given again good harvests and bread to the land of Judah, and she rose up to go from Moab back to her own land and her own town of Bethlehem. Her two daughters-in-law loved her and both would have gone with her, though the land of Judah was a strange land to them, for they were of the Moabite people.

Naomi said to them, "Go back, my daughters, to your own mothers' homes. May the Lord deal kindly with you, as you have been kind to your husbands and to me. May the Lord grant that each of you may yet find another husband and a happy home." Then Naomi kissed them in farewell, and the three women all wept together. The two young widows said to her, "You have been a good mother to us, and we will go with you, and live among your people."

"No, no," said Naomi. "You are young and I am old. Go back and be happy among your own people."

Then Orpah kissed Naomi and went back to her people, but Ruth would not leave her. She said, "Do not ask me to leave you, for I never will. Where you go, I will go; where you live, I will live; your people shall be my people; and your God shall be my God. Where you die, I will die, and be buried. Nothing but death itself shall part you and me."

When Naomi saw that Ruth was firm in her purpose, she ceased trying to persuade her; so the two women went together. They walked around the Dead Sea, and crossed the river Jordan, and climbed the mountains of Judah, and came to Bethlehem.

Naomi had been absent from Bethlehem for ten years, but her friends were all glad to see her again. They said, "Is this Naomi, whom we knew years ago?" Now the name *Naomi* means "pleasant." And Naomi said:

"Call me not Naomi; call me Mara, for the Lord has made my life bitter. I went out full, with my husband and two sons; now I come home empty, without them. Do not call me 'Pleasant'; call me 'Bitter.'" The name *"Mara,"* by which Naomi wished to be called, means "bitter." But Naomi learned later that "Pleasant" was the right name for her after all.

There was living in Bethlehem at that time a very rich man named Boaz. He owned large fields that were abundant in their harvests; and he was related to the family of Elimelech, Naomi's husband, who had died.

It was the custom in Israel when they reaped the grain not to gather all the stalks, but to leave some for the poor people, who followed after the reapers with their sickles, and gathered what was left. When Naomi and Ruth came to Bethlehem it was the time of the barley harvest; and Ruth went out into the fields to glean the grain which the reapers had left. It so happened that she was gleaning in the field that belonged to Boaz, this rich man.

Boaz came out from the town to see his men reaping, and he said to them, "The Lord be with you"; and they answered him,

"The Lord bless you." And Boaz said to his master of the reapers, "Who is this young woman that I see gleaning in the field?"

The man answered, "It is the young woman from the land of Moab, who came with Naomi. She asked leave to glean after the reapers and has been here gathering grain since yesterday."

Then Boaz said to Ruth, "Listen to me, my daughter. Do not go to any other field, but stay here with my young women. No one shall harm you; and when you are thirsty, go and drink at our vessels of water."

Then Ruth bowed to Boaz, and thanked him for his kindness, all the more because she was a stranger in Israel. Boaz said:

"I have heard how true you have been to your mother-in-law, Naomi, in leaving your own land and coming with her to this land. May the Lord, under whose wings you have come, give you a reward!" And at noon, when they sat down to rest and to eat, Boaz gave her some of the food. And he said to the reapers:

"When you are reaping, leave some of the sheaves for her; and drop out some sheaves from the bundles, where she may gather them."

That evening Ruth showed Naomi how much she had gleaned and told her of the rich man Boaz, who had been so kind to her. And Naomi said, "This man is a near relation of ours. Stay in his fields as long as the harvest lasts." And so Ruth gleaned in the fields of Boaz until the harvest had been gathered.

At the end of the harvest, Boaz held a feast on the threshing floor. And after the feast, by the advice of Naomi, Ruth went to him, and said to him, "You are a near relation of my husband and of his father, Elimelech. Now will you not do good to us for his sake?"

And when Boaz saw Ruth he loved her; and soon after this he took her as his wife. And Naomi and Ruth went to live in his home, so that Naomi's life was no more bitter, but pleasant. And Boaz and Ruth had a son, whom they named Obed; and later Obed had a son named Jesse; and Jesse was the father of David, the shepherd boy who became king. So Ruth, the young woman of Moab, who chose the people and the God of Israel, became the mother of kings.

The Lover Pleads With His Friend for Old Friends

WILLIAM BUTLER YEATS

We cannot afford to make new friends at the expense of our old ones.

> *Though you are in your shining days,*
> *Voices among the crowd*
> *And new friends busy with your praise,*
> *Be not unkind or proud,*
> *But think about old friends the most:*
> *Time's bitter flood will rise,*
> *Your beauty perish and be lost*
> *For all eyes but these eyes.*

Friendship

This poem reminds us of some of the "rules" of friendship, as well as some of the rewards.

Friendship needs no studied phrases.
Polished face, or winning wiles;
Friendship deals no lavish praises,
Friendship dons no surface smiles.

Friendship follows Nature's diction,
Shuns the blandishments of art.
Boldly severs truth from fiction,
Speaks the language of the heart.

Friendship favors no condition,
Scorns a narrow-minded creed,
Lovingly fulfills its mission,
Be it word or be it deed.

Friendship cheers the faint and weary,
Makes the timid spirit brave,
Warns the erring, lights the dreary,
Smooths the passage to the grave.

Friendship—pure, unselfish friendship,

All through life's allotted span,
Nurtures, strengthens, widens, lengthens,
Man's relationship with man.

The Bear and the Travelers

AESOP

Fair-weather friends were around in the days of Aesop, in
the sixth century B.C., and they still abound today. Everyone
should learn how to recognize and how not to be one.

Two travelers were on the road together, when a Bear suddenly
appeared on the scene. Before he observed them, one made for a
tree at the side of the road and climbed up into the branches and
hid there. The other was not so nimble as his companion; and as he
could not escape, he threw himself on the ground and pretended to
be dead. The Bear came up and sniffed all round him, but he kept
perfectly still and held his breath; for they say that a bear will not
touch a dead body. The Bear took him for a corpse and went away.
When the coast was clear, the Traveler in the tree came down and
asked the other what it was the Bear had whispered to him when he
put his mouth to his ear. The other replied, "He told me never again
to travel with a friend who deserts you at the first sign of danger."

Misfortune tests the sincerity of friendship.

WORK

Work

As you grow older, you find that work of one kind or another takes up a greater and greater part of your life. The school day gets longer. Homework assignments get harder and more time-consuming. Your parents ask you to begin to take on a few more household chores. Eventually you begin to take summer jobs. Meanwhile, hopefully, you make time to do some volunteer work for those less fortunate than you.

You are discovering that work is a necessary, unavoidable fact of life. And you are learning that, generally speaking, no one else is going to do your work for you, as we see in Aesop's fable of "Hercules and the Wagoner." The first English settlers in this country learned that lesson, too. Many of them were "gentlemen" who weren't used to working very hard in England, and they brought their habits with them to Jamestown, Virginia. Their motivation wasn't very high until their leader, Captain John Smith, announced a new rule. Those who did not pitch in and help would not get a share of the colony's food. In other words, if you don't work, you don't eat. Suddenly, many more people became a lot more motivated.

As you spend more time working, you will naturally spend less time playing. Don't be alarmed. It does not mean life gets less enjoyable. In fact, if you approach your work in the right way, just the opposite is true. Life will be richer, fuller, and, yes, more fun. That's because work brings all sorts of rewards. Obviously, it can bring monetary reward, as we see in another Aesop story, "The Farmer and His Sons." But Aesop has more in mind than just the money. He is also pointing to the satisfaction of a job well done. There are few experiences more enjoyable than such satisfaction, and those who miss it are missing one of the best parts of life.

The attitude you take in approaching your work is all-important, both in terms of doing the job well and in terms of whether or not you are going to enjoy it. It can be done thoroughly or carelessly, cheerfully or with bad temper. It's up to you. The mistake many people make is not realizing that it's usually not the work itself but the attitude you bring to the work that makes it a good or bad experience.

Another mistake people make is trying to avoid work because they think that somehow life will be better without it. The truth is, most people find life without work boring, as we see in the tale "A Week of Sundays." And life without work makes most people feel worthless. Work brings dignity to life, as we see in the story of John Henry.

Of course, some work is simply unpleasant. We'd rather not have to do it, but we have no choice, so the best course is to buckle down and get it over with. Even here, though, there is an important lesson to be heeded. Since life is full of work, it makes sense, when possible, to choose the kind of work we like, even love.

For most people, that idea is an important key to satisfaction in life. Remember that the word *vocation* comes from the Latin root "to call." Hopefully your vocation—your life's work—will be a calling, something you love to spend your time doing. For the Wright Brothers, a fascination with tinkering in their Ohio bicycle shop led them to Kitty Hawk, North Carolina. As they showed us, a love of labor leads to some of life's greatest joys and accomplishments.

Hercules and the Wagoner
AESOP

Sometimes we should complain less and work more.

A wagoner was driving his team along a muddy lane with a full load behind them, when the wheels of his wagon sank so deep in the mire that no efforts of his horses could move them. As he stood there, looking helplessly on and calling loudly at intervals upon Hercules for assistance, the god himself appeared and said to him, "Put your shoulder to the wheel, man, and goad on your horses, and then you may call on Hercules to assist you. If you won't lift a finger to help yourself, you can't expect Hercules or anyone else to come to your aid."

Heaven helps those who help themselves.

Hercules Cleans the Augean Stables

The cleaning of the Augean stables was the fifth of the famous Twelve Labors of Hercules, which the great Greek hero performed by order of his cousin, King Eurystheus of Mycenae. We usually think of Hercules for his strength, but here we admire his intelligence as much as his brute force in tackling a nearly impossible job.

The fifth labor of Hercules was the famous cleaning of the Augean stables. Augeas, the king of Elis, had a herd of three thousand cattle, and he had built a stable miles long for them. Year after year his herd kept growing, and he could not get enough men to take care of the barns. The cows could hardly get into them because of the filth, or if they did get in, they were never quite sure of getting out again because the dirt was piled so high. It was said the stables had not been cleaned in thirty years.

Hercules told Augeas he would clean the barns in one day if the king would give him one tenth of all his cows. Augeas thought the great hero could never do it in so short a time, so he made the agreement in the presence of his young son.

The king's stables were near the two rivers Alpheus and Peneus. Hercules cut a great channel to bring the two streams together and then run into the stables. They rushed along and carried the dirt out so quickly the king could not believe it. He did not intend to pay the reward, so he pretended he had never made a promise.

The dispute was taken before a court for the judges to decide. Hercules called the little prince as a witness, and the boy told the truth about it, which caused the king to fall into such a rage he sent both his son and Hercules out of the country. So Hercules left the land of Elis and continued his twelve labors, but his heart was filled with contempt for the faithless king.

Kill Devil Hill

HARRY COMBS

Here is one of the all-time great American success stories. A childhood fascination with a toy helicopter powered by rubber bands ultimately led Wilbur (1867-1912) and Orville (1871-1948) Wright to what can only be described as one of mankind's most spectacular achievements. In 1900 the Wright brothers began taking their gliders to Kitty Hawk, on North Carolina's Outer Banks, because the ocean breezes and lofty dunes were an ideal environment for testing their odd-looking flying contraptions. On December 17, 1903, numerous experiments and several "failures" later, Orville made the first powered flight of 120 feet. Wilbur, in the fourth and longest flight of the day, described below, made 852 feet in 59 seconds. If ever we need inspiration as we toil toward some distant, elusive goal, surely we find it here. Here is great work begun by genius, but finished by labor.

The people of Kitty Hawk had always been generous and kind to Wilbur and Orville—friendly and warm, sharing their food and worldly goods, sparing no effort to assist in any way they could to provide physical comfort, and open in their respect for the brothers. Most of them, however, felt less convinced about the Wrights' ability to fly; Kitty Hawk was an area where the reaction to flight was often expressed in such familiar bits of folk wisdom as "If

God had wanted man to fly, He would have given him wings."

Bill Tate, who from the beginning had been a close friend to the Wrights, was not present at the camp on December 17, 1903. This was not a sign of lack of faith; he had assumed that "no one but a crazy man would attempt to fly in such a wind."

The brothers had different ideas. Shortly before twelve o'clock, for the fourth attempt of the day, Wilbur took his position on the flying machine, the engine sputtering and clattering in its strange thunder. His peaked cap was pulled snug across his head, and the wind blowing across the flats reached him with a sandpapery touch. As he had felt it do before, the machine trembled in the gusts, rocking from side to side on the sixty-foot launching track. He settled himself in the hip cradle, feet snug behind him, hands on the controls, studying the three instrument gauges. He looked to each side to be certain no one was near the wings. There were no assistants to hold the wings as they had done with the gliders, for Wilbur believed that unless a man was skilled in what he was doing he ought not touch anything, and he had insisted on a free launch, for he knew the craft would require only forty feet in the stiff wind to lift itself into the air.

Wilbur shifted his head to study the beach area. Today was different. The wintry gale had greatly reduced the bird population, as far as he could see. It had been that way since they awoke. Very few of the familiar seagulls were about beneath the leaden skies.

Wilbur turned to each side again, looked at his brother, and nodded. Everything was set, and Wilbur reached to the restraining control and pulled the wire free. Instantly, the machine rushed forward and, as he expected, was forty feet down the track when he eased into the air. He had prepared himself for almost every act of the wind, but the gusts were too strong, and he was constantly correcting and overcorrecting. The hundred-foot mark fell behind as the aircraft lunged up and down like a winged bull. Then he was two hundred feet from the start of his run, and the pitch motions were even more violent. The aircraft seemed to stagger as it struck a sudden downdraft and darted toward the sands. Only a foot above the ground Wilbur regained control, and eased it back up.

Three hundred feet—and the bucking motions were easing off.

And then the five witnesses and Orville were shouting and gesturing wildly, for it was clear that Wilbur had passed some invisible wall in the sky and had regained control. Four hundred feet out, he was still holding the safety altitude of about fifteen feet above the ground, and the airplane was flying smoother now, no longer darting and lunging about, just easing with the gusts between an estimated eight and fifteen feet.

The seconds ticked away and it was a quarter of a minute since Wilbur had started, and there was no question, now: the machine was under control and was sustaining itself by its own power.

It was flying.

The moment had come. It was here, now.

Five hundred feet.

Six hundred.

Seven hundred!

My God, he's trying to reach Kitty Hawk itself, nearly four miles away! And indeed, this is just what Wilbur was trying to do, for he kept heading toward the houses and trees still well before him.

Eight hundred feet. . .

Still going; still flying. Ahead of him, a rise in the ground, a sprawling hump, a hummock of sand. Wilbur brought the elevator into position to raise the nose, to gain altitude to clear the hummock; for beyond this point lay clear sailing, good flying, and he was lifting, the machine rising slowly. But hummocks do strange things to winds blowing at such high speeds. The wind soared up from the sands, rolling and tumbling, and reached out invisibly to push the flying machine downward. The nose dropped too sharply; Wilbur brought it up; and instantly the oscillations began again, a rapid jerking up and down of the nose. The winds were simply too much, the ground-induced roll too severe, and the *Flyer* "suddenly darted into the ground," as Orville later described it.

They knew as they ran that the impact was greater than that of an intentional landing. The skids dug in, and all the weight of the aircraft struck hard, and above the wind they heard the wood splinter and crack. The aircraft bounced once, borne as much by the wind as by its own momentum, and settled back to the sands, the forward elevator braces askew, broken so that the surfaces hung at an angle. Unhurt, aware that he had been flying a marvelously long time, mildly disappointed at not having continued his flight, stuck in the sand with the wind blowing into his face and the engine grinding out its now familiar clattering, banging roar, Wilbur reached out to shut off power. The propellers whistled and whirred as they slowed, the sounds of the chains came to him more clearly, and then only the wind could be heard. The wind, the sand hissing against fabric and his own clothes and across the ground, and perhaps a gull or two, and certainly the beating of his own heart.

It had happened.

He had flown for fifty-nine seconds.

The distance across the surface from his start to his finish was 852 feet.

The air distance, computing airspeed and wind and all the other factors—more than half a mile.

He—they—had done it.

The air age was *now*.

Just fifty-six days before, Simon Newcomb, the only American scientist since Benjamin Franklin to be an associate of the Institute of France, in an article in *The Independent* had shown by "unassailable logic" that human flight was impossible.

They ran up to the machine, where Wilbur stood waiting for them. No one ever recorded what Wilbur's words were at that moment, and no amount of research has been able to unearth them. It is unfortunate, but they are lost forever. . . .

Orville and Wilbur, stiff with cold, went to their living quarters, where they prepared and ate lunch. They rested for several minutes, washed their dishes, and, ready at last to send word of their achievement, at about two o'clock in the afternoon began the walk to the weather station four miles distant in Kitty Hawk. From the station, still run by Joseph J. Dosher, they could dispatch a wire via government facilities to Norfolk, where the message would be continued by telephone to a commercial telegraph office near Dayton. The message, as it was received in Dayton, read:

176 C KA CS 33 PAID.   VIA NORFOLK VA
KITTY LAWK N C DEC 17
BISHOP M WRIGHT
    7 HAWTHORNE ST
SUCCESS FOUR FLIGHTS THURSDAY MORN-
ING ALL AGAINST TWENTY ONE MILE WIND
STARTED FROM LEVEL WITH ENGINE POWER
ALONE AVERAGE SPEED THROUGH AIR
THIRTY ONE MILES LONGEST 57 SECONDS
INFORM PRESS HOME ##### CHRISTMAS.
                    OREVELLE WRIGHT 525P

While this slightly garbled message was being transmitted, including the error of flight time of fifty-seven seconds rather than fifty-nine, the brothers went to the life-saving station nearby to talk with the crew on duty. Captain S.J. Payne, who skippered the facility, told the Wrights he had watched through binoculars as they soared over the ground.

Orville and Wilbur went on to the post office, where they visited Captain and Mrs. Hobbs, who had hauled materials and done other work for them, spent some time with a Dr. Cogswell, and then started their trek back to their camp. It would take them several days to dismantle and pack their *Flyer* into a barrel and two boxes, along with personal gear, and they went to work with their usual thoroughness. It was a strange and quiet aftermath, and several times they went back outside to stand and look at the ground over which they had flown.

Mr. Meant-To

Hear the famous words of Benjamin Franklin: "One today is worth two tomorrows; never leave that till tomorrow which you can do today."

Mr. Meant-To has a comrade,
And his name is Didn't-Do;
Have you ever chanced to meet them?
Did they ever call on you?
These two fellows live together
In the house of Never-Win,
And I'm told that it is haunted
By the ghost of Might-Have-Been.

Results and Roses

EDGAR GUEST

Efforts bring roses, laziness nothing.

The man who wants a garden fair,
Or small or very big,
With flowers growing here and there,
Must bend his back and dig.

The things are mighty few on earth
That wishes can attain,
Whate'er we want of any worth
We've got to work to gain.

It matters not what goal you seek
Its secret here reposes:
You've got to dig from week to week
To get Results or Roses.

The Ballad of John Henry

The John Henry of American folklore was an African-American railroad worker celebrated for his feats of great strength and skill. His most famous exploit was his classic man-versus-machine battle against the new steam drill, which threatened to take the place of the "steel-drivin'" men who hammered long steel bits into solid rock to make holes for dynamite. The story is said to be based on the digging of the Big Bend Tunnel for the Chesapeake and Ohio Railroad in West Virginia's Allegheny Mountains in the 1870's. It is a great American tale of pride and dignity in work.

John Henry was a little baby boy
You could hold him in the palm of your hand.

He gave a long and lonesome cry,
"Gonna be a steel-drivin' man, Lawd, Lawd,
Gonna be a steel-drivin' man."
They took John Henry to the tunnel,
Put him in the lead to drive,
The rock was so tall, John Henry so small,
That he laid down his hammer and he cried,
"Lawd, Lawd,"
Laid down his hammer and he cried.

John Henry started on the right hand,
The steam drill started on the left,
"Fo' I'd let that steam drill beat me down,
I'd hammer my fool self to death, Lawd, Lawd,
Hammer my fool self to death."
John Henry told his captain,
"A man ain't nothin' but a man,
Fo' I let your steam drill beat me down
I'll die with this hammer in my hand, Lawd, Lawd,
Die with this hammer in my hand."
Now the captain told John Henry,
"I believe my tunnel's sinkin' in."
"Stand back, Captain, and doncha be afraid,
That's nothin' but my hammer catchin' wind,
Lawd, Lawd,
That's nothin' but my hammer catchin' wind."

———

John Henry told his cap'n,
"Look yonder, boy, what do I see?
Your drill's done broke and your hole's done choke,
And you can't drive steel like me, Lawd, Lawd,
You can't drive steel like me."

John Henry hammerin' in the mountain,
Till the handle of his hammer caught on fire,
He drove so hard till he broke his po' heart,
Then he laid down his hammer and he died,
Lawd, Lawd,
He laid down his hammer and he died.

They took John Henry to the tunnel,
And they buried him in the sand,
An' every locomotive come rollin' by
Say, "There lies a steel-drivin' man, Lawd, Lawd,
There lies a steel-drivin' man."

The Farmer and His Sons
AESOP

A farmer, being at death's door and desiring to impart to his sons a secret of much moment, called them round him and said, "My sons, I am shortly about to die. I would have you know, therefore, that in my vineyard there lies a hidden treasure. Dig, and you will find it." As soon as their father was dead, the sons took spade and fork and turned up the soil of the vineyard over and over again, in their search for the treasure which they supposed to lie buried there. They found none, however: but the vines, after so thorough a digging, produced a crop such as had never before been seen.

There is no treasure without toil.

The Poor Man and His Seeds

This tale from East Africa reminds us that unexpected reward often has more to do with hard work than with luck.

There was once a poor man who possessed only a very small plot of land and one small bag of seeds. When his field was ready for planting, he rose at sunrise and carefully began to sow his meager crop. At mid-day, when the sun was beating fiercely on his shoulders, he stopped by a tree stump to rest. As he sat, a handful of seeds spilled out of his bag and fell down a hole under the stump.

"Well, they can do no growing down there," the man sighed. "I cannot afford to lose even these few."

So he took a shovel and began digging at the roots of the stump. The day grew hotter, and the sweat ran from his back and brow, but he kept digging. When he finally reached his seeds, he found them lying on top of a buried box. And inside the box he found gold— enough gold coins to make him rich for the rest of his life!

Afterward, people would say to him, "You must be the luckiest man alive."

"Yes, I was lucky," he would say. "I was in my field by sunrise, I dug throughout the hot day, and I did not waste a single seed."

The Rebellion Against the Stomach

We find variations of this story all over the world. Aesop told it as one of his fables. Paul used it in his first letter to the Corinthians. Shakespeare employed it in his play Coriolanus. It teaches two lessons. First, most of us are better off worrying about our own jobs than criticizing others. Second, many big jobs require the cooperation of many workers.

Once a man had a dream in which his hands and feet and mouth and brain all began to rebel against his stomach.

"You good-for-nothing sluggard!" the hands said. "We work all day long, sawing and hammering and lifting and carrying. By evening we're covered with blisters and scratches, and our joints ache, and we're covered with dirt. And meanwhile you just sit there, hogging all the food."

"We agree!" cried the feet. "Think how sore we get, walking back and forth all day long. And you just stuff yourself full, you greedy pig, so that you're that much heavier to carry about."

"That's right!" whined the mouth. "Where do you think all that food you love comes from? I'm the one who has to chew it all up, and as soon as I'm finished you suck it all down for yourself. Do you call that fair?"

"And what about me?" called the brain. "Do you think it's easy being up here, having to think about where your next meal is going to come from? And yet I get nothing at all for my pains."

And one by one the parts of the body joined the complaint against the stomach, which didn't say anything at all.

"I have an idea," the brain finally announced. "Let's all rebel against this lazy belly, and stop working for it."

"Superb idea!" all the other members and organs agreed. "We'll teach you how important we are, you pig. Then maybe you'll do a little work of your own."

So they all stopped working. The hands refused to do any lifting or carrying. The feet refused to walk. The mouth promised not to chew or swallow a single bite. And the brain swore it wouldn't come up with any more bright ideas. At first the stomach growled a bit, as it always did when it was hungry. But after a while it was quiet.

Then, to the dreaming man's surprise, he found he could not walk. He could not grasp anything in his hands. He could not even open his mouth. And he suddenly began to feel rather ill.

The dream seemed to go on for several days. As each day

passed, the man felt worse and worse. "This rebellion had better not last much longer," he thought to himself, "or I'll starve."

Meanwhile, the hands and feet and mouth and brain just lay there, getting weaker and weaker. At first they roused themselves just enough to taunt the stomach every once in a while, but before long they didn't even have the energy for that.

Finally the man heard a faint voice coming from the direction of his feet.

"It could be that we were wrong," they were saying. "We suppose the stomach might have been working in his own way all along."

"I was just thinking the same thing," murmured the brain. "It's true he's been getting all the food. But it seems he's been sending most of it right back to us."

"We might as well admit our error," the mouth said. "The stomach has just as much work to do as the hands and feet and brain and teeth."

"Then let's all get back to work," they cried together. And at that the man woke up.

To his relief, he discovered his feet could walk again. His hands could grasp, his mouth could chew, and his brain could now think clearly. He began to feel much better.

"Well, there's a lesson for me," he thought as he filled his stomach at breakfast. "Either we all work together, or nothing works at all."

The Village Blacksmith
HENRY WADSWORTH LONGFELLOW

Longfellow said that he wrote this poem in praise of an ancestor, and that it was suggested to him by a blacksmith shop beneath a horse chestnut tree near his house in Cambridge, Massachusetts. Here is the character of true, honest, willing labor. It is surely one of the most appealing images in American verse.

Under a spreading chestnut tree
The village smithy stands;
The smith, a mighty man is he,
With large and sinewy hands;
And the muscles of his brawny arms
Are strong as iron bands.
His hair is crisp, and black, and long,
His face is like the tan;
His brow is wet with honest sweat,
He earns whate'er he can,
And looks the whole world in the face,
For he owns not any man.

Week in, week out, from morn till night,
You can hear his bellows blow;
You can hear him swing his heavy sledge,
With measured beat and slow,

Like a sexton ringing the village bell,
When the evening sun is low.

And children coming home from school
Look in at the open door;
They love to see the flaming forge,
And hear the bellows roar;
And catch the burning sparks that fly
Like chaff from a threshing floor.
He goes on Sunday to the church,
And sits among his boys;
He hears the parson pray and preach,
He hears his daughter's voice,
Singing in the village choir,
And it makes his heart rejoice.

It sounds to him like her mother's voice,
Singing in Paradise!
He needs must think of her once more,
How in the grave she lies;
And with his hard, rough hand he wipes
A tear out of his eyes.

Toiling—rejoicing—sorrowing
Onward through life he goes;
Each morning sees some task begin,
Each evening sees it close;

Something attempted, something done,
Has earned a night's repose.

Thanks, thanks to thee, my worthy friend,
For the lesson thou hast taught!
Thus at the flaming forge of life
Our fortunes must be wrought;
Thus on its sounding anvil shaped
Each burning deed and thought!

The Week of Sundays

In this old tale we see the difference between idle time, which we steal, and leisure time, which we earn. The truth is that people who never have anything to do are usually the most dissatisfied because they are the most bored. Our leisure time, on the other hand, we enjoy largely because we've put plenty of work behind us to get it.

Once upon a time there was a man named Bobby O'Brien who never did a stitch of work in his life unless he absolutely had to.

"Come now, Bobby," his friends used to say, "what's so wrong with a little hard work? You'd think it was the black plague itself, the way you guard yourself against it."

"My friends, I have no more against work than the next man,"

Bobby would reply. "In fact, nothing fascinates me more than work. I can sit here and watch it all day, if you'll only give me the chance."

And of course, he was perfectly useless around the house.

"Aren't you ashamed of yourself, now?" his wife, Katie, moaned one afternoon. "A fine example you're setting for the children! Do you want them to grow up to be lazy slobs too?"

"It's Sunday, my dear, the day of rest," Bobby pointed out. "Now why would you want to be disturbing it? If you want my opinion, it's the only day out of the whole week worth getting out of bed for. The only problem with Sunday is that as soon as it's over, the rest of the week starts up again." Bobby was a great philosopher, having so much time on his hands.

That very night the whole family was sitting around the fire, waiting for their soup to boil, when what should they hear but a tap-tap-tap at the window. Bobby strolled over and raised the sash, and into the room hopped a little man no bigger than a strutting rooster.

"I was just passing by," the wee man said, "and smelled something good and strong, and thought I might have a bite to eat."

"You're welcome to as much as you want," Bobby said, thinking that such a little man couldn't possibly hold more than a spoonful or two. So the tiny fellow sat down at the fireside, but no sooner had Katie given him a steaming bowl than he slurped it down and asked for another. Katie gave him seconds, and he swallowed that one faster than the first. She gave him thirds, and he drained the bowl almost before she had filled it up.

"What a little pig," Bobby thought to himself. "He'll have all of our suppers, before he's through. Still, I asked him in, and he is our guest, so we must hold our tongues."

After five or six bowls the little man smacked his lips and jumped off his stool.

"It's most kind you've been," he laughed. "A more hospitable family I've never met. Now I must be on my way, but as a way of thanks I'll be more than happy to grant the next wish uttered aloud beneath this roof." And with that he hopped through the window and vanished into the night.

Well, everyone wanted to wish for something different. One child wanted a bag of sweets, and the other child wanted a box of toys. Katie thought a new bed would be nice, as the old one was showing signs of collapse. Bobby could name a dozen or so things he'd like to have, right off the top of his head, perhaps a new fishing pole, or maybe a chocolate cake.

"We need more time to think it over," he declared. "The trouble is, tomorrow's Monday morning, and there'll be work and chores to get in the way of our thinking. I wish we had a week of Sundays, and then we could take our time and figure it out."

"Now you've done it!" Katie cried. "You've gone and wasted our only wish on a week of Sundays! You might have wished for a few more brains in that thick head of yours before you opened your mouth for a wish like that!"

"Well, well, it's not such a bad wish, you know," said Bobby, who was just now realizing what he had done. "A week of Sundays will be a fine thing, after all. I've been needing a little rest, and this will give me the chance."

"Rest is the last thing you need, you lazy bag of bones," Katie moaned, hustling the children off to bed.

But the next morning when Bobby woke up to hear the churchbells pealing, and he remembered he had seven whole days before him of not having a thing in the world to do, he decided he'd made the wisest of all possible wishes. He lolled around bed all morning, while Katie took the children to church, and didn't bother to rouse himself until he finally smelled a nice plump chicken coming out of the oven for Sunday dinner.

"What a remarkable event!" He yawned and stretched as he sat down at the table. "King Solomon himself could never have wished for such a wonderful thing as a week of Sundays." And after he stuffed himself, he wandered outside and took a nap beneath his favorite tree.

The next day he lay in bed all morning again, and got up only when church was safely over. But the only thing Katie put on the table was a few chicken bones left from the day before, when Bobby had eaten the whole Sunday dinner. The next day was even worse. Bobby sat down with a roaring appetite, only to find porridge and potatoes gracing the table.

"Now what kind of dinner is this?" he asked. "Have you forgotten what day of the week it is? Porridge and potatoes aren't fit for Sunday, my dear."

"And what else did you expect?" Katie cried. "How am I supposed to buy a new chicken with every shop in the village closed for seven straight days? It's all we have in the cupboard, so you'd better get used to it, my good man."

Well, the next morning Bobby's stomach was growling so fiercely he couldn't help but getting out of bed a little earlier than his usual Sunday custom. He wandered around the kitchen a bit, checking here and there for a bite to eat, but he found only a loaf of stale bread in the pantry.

"You know, my dear," he said, "I've been thinking I need a bit of exercise. I believe I'll go out to the garden and dig a few potatoes for dinner."

"You'll do nothing of the sort," Katie snapped. "I won't have you digging potatoes on Sunday morning, with the neighbors passing by on their way to church. That won't do at all."

"But there's nothing in the house but bits of stale bread," Bobby cried.

"And who do you have to blame but yourself and your week of Sundays for that?" Katie asked.

The next day Bobby was up at the crack of dawn, pacing back and forth across the house and drumming his fingers on every windowsill. The children followed him everywhere he went until the churchbells began to peal, and then they bawled and whimpered to no end.

"What's wrong with these young ones?" Bobby whined. "Have all their manners gone and left them?"

"And what do you expect, after all?" Katie cried. "The poor little things have sat through more sermons in a week now than you've snored through all year. Their backs are sore from living in pews, and they've tossed every last penny they've been saving into that collection plate."

"They should be in school, that's where," Bobby declared.

"And who, may I ask, is to blame for that?" Katie inquired.

On the sixth Sunday, Bobby was so fidgety and bored, he decided to go to church with the rest of the family. Every head in the congregation swung around when he came through the door and crept up the aisle.

"There's the man!" the preacher cried from the pulpit. "Here's the rascal who's kept me up every night this week, wracking my poor brain for another new sermon! Here's the troublemaker who's ruined every last throat in the choir, and almost worn the fingers off the poor organist! I guess you've come to survey your dirty work now, have you?"

And when the service was over, Bobby found his neighbors lined up to greet him.

"Well, now," asked one, "did you stop to think of how we're to bring in the harvest with so many Sundays getting in the way?"

"And how are the rest of us to make a living, having to keep our doors closed all week?" asked the butcher and the baker.

"And what about the washing and ironing and mending?" someone called. "Do you know how much is piled up for next Monday, should it ever come again?"

"And by the way," said the schoolmaster, "have you been taking care of your children's lessons, or have they forgotten how to read and write by now?"

Bobby made his way home as fast as he could.

"Thank goodness there's only one Sunday left!" he sighed as

soon as he was safe behind his own door. "Any more would be dangerous to a man's health."

That last Sunday was the longest day of Bobby O'Brien's life. The minutes passed like hours, and the hours stretched into eternities. Bobby twiddled his thumbs, and stood on one foot, and walked in circles, and watched the clock.

"Is this thing broken?" he cried, grabbing it from the mantel and shaking it till its insides rattled. "You can't tell me the time has ever dragged by so slow!"

"When have you ever wanted a Sunday to end?" Katie asked. "Aren't you forgetting that tomorrow is Monday?"

"Forgetting it? It's all I can think about," Bobby exclaimed. "I've never in my life looked forward to any day as much as this Monday morning."

The shadows slowly crept across the lawn, the sun finally went down, and just as the first star popped into the sky, who should come rapping at the window but the same little man who visited one week ago.

"And how did you enjoy your wish?" he asked Bobby.

"Not very much, I'm afraid," said Bobby.

"Really?" exclaimed the little man. "Then you wouldn't want to trade another bite to eat for another week of Sundays?"

"For goodness' sake, no!" cried Bobby. "The only days of rest I want are the ones I've worked six days to earn. It took me all week to learn that lesson, and I won't be forgetting it anytime soon. So I'll thank you to be gone with your wishes, my friend."

And at that the little man disappeared and was never seen again.

COURAGE

Courage

The most common misunderstanding about courage is the belief that courage means not feeling afraid. In truth, courage is not at all about emotions. It is not about how you feel. It's about how you *act*.

Everybody is afraid of something—it's perfectly normal. You might be scared of being alone in a strange place, or asking someone out on a date, or saying the wrong thing and having people laugh at you. Feeling fear is an unavoidable part of life.

The question is, what do you *do* when you have those fears? Do you run and hide? Or do you stand and face the situation?

This is the essence of courage—mustering the strength and will to do what you know you should do, even though you are afraid. The great philosopher Aristotle put it this way: "We become brave by doing brave acts." He meant that we may not *feel* very brave when we do something courageous. Nevertheless, by *acting* brave, by doing what is right and required, we turn ourselves into courageous people. It's the only way to overcome fear.

So courage requires practice. One step at a time, little by little, you have to try facing your fears and acting the way you know you should act. And as you practice, some of your fears will go away. Here is a part of life where it makes sense to reach higher and higher. When you do, you'll find you have more courage than you thought.

Courage also requires wisdom. That is, you have to know the things you fear as well as the way you need to act to face those fears. You'll need the virtue of honesty for that—honesty with yourself.

As you'll see in this chapter, there are many different kinds of true courage. There is the kind that stays cool and calm in troubled times, as in the story of Dolley Madison. There is the courage that stands up for what is right, as Rosa Parks and Susan B. Anthony did. There is the courage of acting according to your faith in God, as David did when he fought Goliath. And there is the courage of trusting yourself and refusing to follow the crowd when the crowd is wrong, as Rudyard Kipling tells us in his poem "If—." But there are also varieties of false courage, too, and you should always guard against them. Simply being loud and talking as if you are brave is one kind. We see it in the story of "Chanticleer and Partlet," and we see how it often rises from our own vanity. The strong beating up the weak is another kind of false courage. It's really cowardice, as we see in the story "The Leopard's Revenge." And there is nothing courageous about taking stupid, unnecessary risks just for thrills or to show off. Again, true courage requires wisdom—the wisdom of being able to distinguish between those circumstances you fear but need to face and those circumstances you fear and rightly need to avoid.

An Appeal from the Alamo

WILLIAM BARRET TRAVIS

The Alamo in San Antonio, Texas, has become an American symbol of unyielding courage and self-sacrifice. A force of Texans captured the mission fort in late 1835 after the outbreak of revolution against the dictatorship of Mexican General Antonio Lopez de Santa Anna. By early 1836, Lieutenant Colonel William Barret Travis and the fort's garrison found themselves hemmed in by a Mexican army swelling to 6,000 troops. On February 24, Travis dispatched couriers to nearby Texas towns, carrying frantic appeals for aid. Fewer than three dozen men picked their way through enemy lines to join the Alamo's defenders. The siege continued until March 6, when Santa Anna's forces overwhelmed the fort. The entire garrison was killed, some 180 men, including Colonel Travis, James Bowie, and Davy Crockett.

COMMANDANCY OF THE ALAMO, TEXAS

February 24, 1836

To the People of Texas and
All Americans in the World.

FELLOW CITIZENS AND COMPATRIOTS

I am besieged by a thousand or more of the Mexicans under Santa Anna. I have sustained a continual bombardment and cannonade for twenty-four hours and have not lost a man. The enemy has demanded a surrender at discretion; otherwise the garrison are to be put to the sword if the fort is taken. I have answered the demand with a cannon shot, and our flag still waves proudly from the walls. *I shall never surrender nor retreat.* Then, I call on you in the name of Liberty, of patriotism, and of everything dear to the American character, to come to our aid with all dispatch. The enemy is receiving reinforcements daily and will no doubt increase to three or four thousand in four or five days. If this call is neglected, I am determined to sustain myself as long as possible and die like a soldier who never forgets what is due to his own honor and that of his country.

VICTORY OR DEATH

WILLIAM BARRET TRAVIS
Lieutenant Colonel, Commandant

Chanticleer and Partlet
RETOLD BY J. BERG ESENWEIN
AND MARIETTA STOCKARD

This story comes from "Nun's Priest's Tale," one of Geoffrey Chaucer's Canterbury Tales. It reminds us that there is such a thing as false courage, which may rise from our own vanity.

Once there was a barnyard close to a wood, in a little valley. Here dwelt a cock, Chanticleer by name. His comb was redder than coral, his feathers were like burnished gold, and his voice was wonderful to hear. Long before dawn each morning his crowing sounded over the valley, and his seven wives listened in admiration.

One night as he sat on the perch by the side of Dame Partlet, his most loved mate, he began to make a curious noise in his throat.

"What is it, my dear?" said Dame Partlet. "You sound frightened."

"Oh!" said Chanticleer. "I had the most horrible dream. I thought that as I roamed down by the wood a beast like a dog sprang out and seized me. His color was red, his nose was small, and his eyes were like coals of fire. Ugh! It was fearful!"

"Tut, tut! Are you a coward to be frightened by a dream? You've been eating more than was good for you. I wish my husband to be wise and brave if he would keep my love!" Dame Partlet clucked, as she smoothed her feathers and slowly closed her scarlet eyes. She felt disgusted at having her sleep disturbed.

"Of course you are right, my love, yet I have heard of many dreams which came true. I am sure I shall meet with some misfortune, but we will not talk of it now. I am quite happy to be here by your side. You are very beautiful, my dear!"

Dame Partlet unclosed one eye slowly and made a pleased sound, deep in her throat.

The next morning, Chanticleer flew down from the perch and called his hens about him for their breakfast. He walked about boldly, calling, "Chuck! chuck!" at each grain of corn which he found. He felt very proud as they all looked at him so admiringly. He strutted about in the sunlight, flapping his wings to show off his feathers, and now and then throwing back his head and crowing exultantly. His dream was forgotten; there was no fear in his heart.

Now all this time, Reynard, the fox, was lying hidden in the bushes on the edge of the wood bordering the barnyard. Chanticleer walked nearer and nearer his hiding place. Suddenly he saw a butterfly in the grass, and as he stooped toward it, he spied the fox.

"Cok! cok!" he cried in terror, and turned to flee.

"Dear friend, why do you go?" said Reynard in his gentlest voice. "I only crept down here to hear you sing. Your voice is like an angel's. Your father and mother once visited my house. I should so love to see you there too. I wonder if you remember your father's singing? I can see him now as he stood on tiptoe, stretching out his long slender neck, sending out his glorious voice. He always flapped his wings and closed his eyes before he sang. Do you do it in the same way? Won't you sing just once and let me hear you? I am so anxious to know if you really sing better than your father."

Chanticleer was so pleased with this flattery that he flapped his wings, stood up on tiptoe, shut his eyes, and crowed as loudly as he could.

No sooner had he begun than Reynard sprang forward, caught him by the throat, threw him over his shoulder, and made off toward his den in the woods.

The hens made a loud outcry when they saw Chanticleer

being carried off, so that the people in the cottage nearby heard and ran out after the fox. The dog heard and ran yelping after him. The cow ran, the calf ran, and the pigs began to squeal and run too. The ducks and geese quacked in terror and flew up into the treetops. Never was there heard such an uproar. Reynard began to feel a bit frightened himself.

"How swiftly you do run!" said Chanticleer from his back. "If I were you I should have some sport out of those slow fellows, who are trying to catch you. Call out to them and say, 'Why do you creep along like snails? Look! I am far ahead of you and shall soon be feasting on this cock in spite of all of you!'"

Reynard was pleased at this and opened his mouth to call to his pursuers; but as soon as he did so, the cock flew away from him and perched up in a tree safely out of reach.

The fox saw he had lost his prey and began his old tricks again. "I was only proving to you how important you are in the barnyard. See what a commotion we caused! I did not mean to frighten you. Come down now and we will go along together to my home. I have something very interesting to show you there."

"No, no," said Chanticleer. "You will not catch me again. A man who shuts his eyes when he ought to be looking deserves to lose his sight entirely."

By this time, Chanticleer's friends were drawing near, so Reynard turned to flee. "The man who talks when he should be silent deserves to lose what he has gained," he said as he sped away through the wood.

David and Goliath
RETOLD BY J. BERG ESENWEIN
AND MARIETTA STOCKARD

Here is the famous story of a brave youth who forges his courage through his faith.

Long ago, in the land of Bethlehem, there lived a man named Jesse, who had eight stalwart sons. The youngest of these sons was David.

Even as a little lad, David was ruddy, beautiful of countenance, and strong of body. When his older brothers drove the flocks to the fields, he ran with them. Each day as he leaped over the hillsides and listened to the gurgling water in the brooks and the songs of birds in the trees, he grew stronger of limb and more filled with joy and courage. Sometimes he made songs of the beautiful things he saw and heard. His eye was keen, his hands strong, and his aim sure. When he fitted a stone into his sling, he never missed the mark at which he threw it.

As he grew older, he was given the care of a part of the flocks. One day as he lay on the hillside keeping watch over his sheep, a lion rushed out of the woods and seized a lamb. David leaped to his feet and ran forward. He had no fear in his heart, no thought but to save the lamb. He sprang upon the lion, seized him by his hairy head and, with no weapon but the staff in his strong young hands, he slew him. Another day, a bear came down upon them. Him also, David slew.

Now, soon after this, the Philistines marshaled their armies and came across the hills to drive the children of Israel away from their homes. King Saul gathered his armies and went out to meet them. David's three oldest brothers went with the king, but David was left at home to tend the sheep. "Thou art too young; stay in the fields and keep the flocks safe," they said to David.

Forty days went by, and no news of the battle came; so Jesse [David's father] called David to him and said: "Take this food for thy brethren, and go up to the camp to see how they fare."

David set out early in the morning and journeyed up to the hill on which the army was encamped. There was great shouting and the armies were drawn up in battle array when David arrived. He made his way through the ranks and found his brethren. As he stood talking with them, silence fell upon King Saul's army; and there on the hillside opposite stood a great giant. He strode up and down, his armor glittering in the sun. His shield was so heavy that the strongest man in King Saul's army could not have lifted it, and the sword at his side was so great that the strongest arm could not have wielded it.

"It is the great giant, Goliath," David's brethren told him. "Each day he strides over the hill and calls out his challenge to the men of Israel, but no man amongst us dares to stand before him."

"What! Are the men of Israel afraid?" asked David. "Will they let this Philistine defy the armies of the living God? Will no one go forth to meet him?" He turned from one to another, questioning them.

Eliab, David's oldest brother, heard him and was angry. "Thou art naughty and proud of heart," he said. "Thou has stolen away from home thinking to see a great battle. With whom has thou left the sheep?"

"The keeper hath charge of them; and our father, Jesse, sent me hither; and my heart is glad that I am come," answered David. "I myself will go forth to meet this giant. The God of Israel will go with me, for I have no fear of Goliath nor all of his hosts!"

The men standing near hastened to the tent of King Saul and told him of David's words.

"Let him stand before me," commanded the king.

When David was brought into his presence and Saul saw that he was but a youth, he attempted to dissuade him. But David told him how he had slain the lion and the bear with his naked hands. "The Lord who delivered me from them will deliver me out of the hand of this Philistine," he said.

Then King Saul said: "Go, and the Lord go with thee!"

He had his own armor fetched for David, his helmet of brass, his coat of mail, and his own sword. But David said: "I cannot fight with these. I am not skilled in their use." He put them down, for he knew that each man must win his battles with his own weapons.

Then he took his staff in his hand, his shepherd's bag and sling he hung at his side, and he set out from the camp of Israel. He ran lightly down the hillside, and when he came to the brook which ran at the foot of the hill, he stooped, and choosing five smooth stones from the brook, dropped them into his bag.

The army of King Saul upon one hill, and the host of the Philistines upon the other, looked on in silent wonder. The great giant strode toward David, and when Goliath saw that he was but a youth, ruddy and fair of countenance, his anger knew no bounds.

"Am I a dog, that thou comest to me with sticks?" he shouted. "Do the men of Israel make mock of me to send a child against me? Turn back, or I will give thy flesh to the birds of the air and to the beasts of the field!" Then Goliath cursed David in the name of all his gods.

But no fear came to David's heart. He called out bravely: "Thou comest to me with a sword, and with a spear, and with a shield: But I come to thee in the name of the Lord of hosts, the God of the armies of Israel, whom thou has defied. This day will the Lord deliver thee into mine hands; and I will smite thee, that all the earth may know that there is a God in Israel!"

Then Goliath rushed forward to meet David, and David ran still more swiftly to meet the giant. He put his hand into his bag and took one of the stones from it. He fitted it into his sling, and his keen eye found the place in the giant's forehead where the helmet joined. He drew his sling and, with all the force of his strong right arm, he hurled the stone.

It whizzed through the air and struck deep into Goliath's forehead. His huge body tottered—then fell crashing to the ground. As he lay with his face upon the earth, David ran swiftly to his side, drew forth the giant's own sword, and severed his huge head from his body.

When the army of Israel saw this, they rose up with a great shout and rushed down the hillside to throw themselves upon the frightened Philistines who were fleeing in terror. When they saw their greatest warrior slain by this lad, they fled toward their own land, leaving their tents and all their riches to be spoiled by the men of Israel.

When the battle was ended, King Saul caused David to be brought before him, and he said: "Thou shalt go no more to the house of thy father but thou shalt be as mine own son."

So David stayed in the tents of the king, and at length he was given command over the king's armies. All Israel honored him, and long years after, he was made the king in King Saul's stead.

Dolley Madison Saves the National Pride
DOROTHEA PAYNE MADISON

In August 1814, a British army marched on Washington, D.C., thinking that by burning the American capital it could bring an end to the War of 1812. Panic reigned in the city as the red-coated columns approached. Many public records, including the Declaration of Independence, had already been stuffed into linen bags and carted off to Virginia, where they were piled up in a vacant house. Now the roads leading out of town began to fill with fleeing American soldiers and statesmen as well as wagons loaded with families and their valuables.

Dolley Madison, wife of the fourth president, calmly directed evacuation details at the White House. A large portrait

*of George Washington by Gilbert Stuart hung in the dining
room. It would be an unbearable disgrace if it fell into British hands. Mrs. Madison ordered the doorkeeper and gardener
to bring it along, but the huge frame was screwed so tightly
to the wall that no one could get it down. Minutes ticked by
as they tugged and pulled. At last someone found an ax. They
chopped the frame apart, removed the canvas, and sent it off for
safekeeping. Soon afterward the British entered the District of
Columbia, setting fire to the Capitol and the White House.*

*The rescue of Washington's portrait quickly took its place
as one of America's most cherished acts of heroism. This letter, written by Dolley to her sister, Anna, even as the city
fell, speaks to us of unflinching courage and levelheadedness
amid chaos and retreat.*

Tuesday, August 23, 1814

Dear Sister:

My husband left me yesterday morning to join General
Winder. He inquired anxiously whether I had courage or firmness
to remain in the President's house until his return on the morrow,
or succeeding day, and on my assurance that I had no fear but for
him, and the success of our army, he left, beseeching me to take
care of myself, and of the Cabinet papers, public and private. I
have since received two dispatches from him, written with a pen-
cil. The last is alarming, because he desires I should be ready at a
moment's warning to enter my carriage, and leave the city; that
the enemy seemed stronger than had at first been reported, and it

might happen that they would reach the city with the intention of destroying it. I am accordingly ready; I have pressed as many Cabinet papers into trunks as to fill one carriage; our private property must be sacrificed, as it is impossible to procure wagons for its transportation.

I am determined not to go myself until I see Mr. Madison safe, so that he can accompany me, as I hear of much hostility toward him. Disaffection stalks around us. My friends and acquaintances are all gone, even Colonel C. with his hundred, who were stationed as a guard in this enclosure. French John [a faithful servant], with his usual activity and resolution, offers to spike the cannon at the gate, and lay a train of powder, which would blow up the British, should they enter the house. To this last proposition I positively object, without being able to make him understand why all advantages in war may not be taken.

Wednesday morning, twelve o'clock. Since sunrise I have been turning my spyglass in every direction, and watching with unwearied anxiety, hoping to discover the approach of my dear husband and his friends; but, alas! I can descry only groups of military, wandering in all directions, as if there was a lack of arms, or of spirit to fight for their own fireside.

Three o'clock. Will you believe it, my sister? We have had a battle, or skirmish, near Bladensburg, and here I am still, within sound of the cannon! Mr. Madison comes not. May God protect us! Two messengers, covered with dust, come to bid me fly; but here I mean to wait for him. . . At this late hour a wagon has been procured, and I have had it filled with plate and the most valuable portable articles belonging to the house. Whether it will reach its destination, the "Bank of Maryland," or fall into the hands of British soldiery, events must determine. Our kind friend, Mr. Carroll, has come to hasten my departure, and in a very bad humor with me, because I insist on waiting until the large picture of General Washington is secured, and it requires to be unscrewed from the wall. This process was found too tedious for these perilous moments; I have ordered the frame to be broken, and the canvas taken out. It is done! and the precious portrait placed in the hands of two gentlemen of New York, for safekeeping. And now, dear sister, I must leave this house, or the retreating army will make me a prisoner of it by filling up the road I am directed to take. When I shall again write to you, or where I shall be tomorrow, I cannot tell!

Dolley

Excerpt from the Diary of Anne Frank

Anne Frank was born in Germany in 1929, but in 1933, after Nazis began to persecute Jews, she moved with her family to Amsterdam. In 1942, after the Nazis occupied the Netherlands, the Franks went into hiding in a secret annex behind Anne's father's business. Two years later, they were discovered and arrested. Anne died in a Nazi concentration camp.

Anne's diary, which she addressed as "Kitty," remains one of our most moving testaments to the courage of the human spirit. "Peter," mentioned in this excerpt, was Peter Van Daan, who with his parents had joined the Franks in hiding.

Tuesday, 7 March, 1944

Dear Kitty,

If I think now of my life in 1942, it all seems so unreal. It was quite a different Anne who enjoyed that heavenly existence from the Anne who has grown wise within these walls. Yes, it was a heavenly life. Boy friends at every turn, about twenty friends and acquaintances of my own age, the darling of nearly all the teachers, spoiled from top to toe by Mummy and Daddy, lots of sweets, enough pocket money, what more could one want?

You will certainly wonder by what means I got around all these people. Peter's word "attractiveness" is not altogether true. All the teachers were entertained by my cute answers, my amusing remarks, my smiling face, and my questioning looks. That is all I was—a terrible flirt, coquettish and amusing. I had one or two advantages, which kept me rather in favor. I was industrious, honest, and frank. I would never have dreamed of cribbing from anyone else. I shared my sweets generously, and I wasn't conceited.

Wouldn't I have become rather forward with so much admiration? It was a good thing that in the midst of, at the height of, all this gaiety, I suddenly had to face reality, and it took me at least a year to get used to the fact that there was no more admiration forthcoming.

How did I appear at school? The one who thought of new jokes and pranks, always "king of the castle," never in a bad mood, never a crybaby. No wonder everyone liked to cycle with me, and I got their attentions.

Now I look back at that Anne as an amusing, but very superficial girl, who has nothing to do with the Anne of today. Peter said quite rightly about me: "If ever I saw you, you were always surrounded by two or more boys and a whole troupe of girls. You were always laughing and always the center of everything!"

What is left of this girl? Oh, don't worry, I haven't forgotten how to laugh or to answer back readily. I'm just as good, if not better, at criticizing people, and I can still flirt if . . . I wish. That's not it though, I'd like that sort of life again for an evening, a few days, or even a week; the life which seems so carefree and gay. But at the end of that week, I should be dead beat and would be only too thankful to listen to anyone who began to talk about something sensible. I don't want followers, but friends, admirers who fall not for a flattering smile but for what one does and for one's character.

I know quite well that the circle around me would be much smaller. But what does that matter, as long as one still keeps a few sincere friends?

Yet I wasn't entirely happy in 1942 in spite of everything; I often felt deserted, but because I was on the go the whole day long, I didn't think about it and enjoyed myself as much as I could. Consciously or unconsciously, I tried to drive away the emptiness I felt with jokes and pranks. Now I think seriously about life and what I have to do. One period of my life is over forever. The care-free schooldays are gone, never to return.

I don't even long for them any more; I have outgrown them, I can't just only enjoy myself as my serious side is always there.

I look upon my life up till the New Year, as it were, through a powerful magnifying glass. The sunny life at home, then coming here in 1942, the sudden change, the quarrels, the bickerings. I couldn't understand it, I was taken by surprise, and the only way I could keep up some bearing was by being impertinent.

The first half of 1943: my fits of crying, the loneliness, how I slowly began to see all my faults and shortcomings, which are so great and which seemed much greater then. During the day I deliberately talked about anything and everything that was far-thest from my thoughts, tried to draw Pim to me; but couldn't. Alone I had to face the difficult task of changing myself, to stop the everlasting reproaches, which were so oppressive and which reduced me to such terrible despondency.

Things improved slightly in the second half of the year, I became a young woman and was treated more like a grownup. I started to think, and write stories, and came to the conclusion that the others no longer had the right to throw me about like an india-rubber ball. I wanted to change in accordance with my own desires. But *one* thing that struck me even more was when I realized that even Daddy would never become my confidant over everything. I didn't want to trust anyone but myself any more.

At the beginning of the New Year: the second great change,

my dream. . . . And with it I discovered my longing, not for a girl friend, but for a boy friend. I also discovered my inward happiness and my defensive armor of superficiality and gaiety. In due time I quieted down and discovered my boundless desire for all that is beautiful and good.

And in the evening, when I lie in bed and end my prayers with the words, "I thank you, God, for all that is good and dear and beautiful," I am filled with joy. Then I think about "the good" of going into hiding, of my health and with my whole being of "dearness" of Peter, of that which is still embryonic and impressionable and which we neither of us dare to name or touch, of that which will come sometime; love, the future, happiness and of "the beauty" which exists in the world; the world, nature, beauty and all, all that is exquisite and fine.

I don't think then of all the misery, but of the beauty that still remains. This is one of the things that Mummy and I are so entirely different about. Her counsel when one feels melancholy is: "Think of all the misery in the world and be thankful that you are not sharing in it!" My advice is: "Go outside, to the fields, enjoy nature and the sunshine, go out and try to recapture happiness in yourself and in God. Think of all the beauty that's still left in and around you and be happy!"

I don't see how Mummy's idea can be right, because then how are you supposed to behave if you go through the misery yourself? Then you are lost. On the contrary, I've found that there is always some beauty left—in nature, sunshine, freedom, in yourself; these can all help you. Look at these things, then you find yourself again, and God, and then you regain your balance.

And whoever is happy will make others happy too. He who has courage and faith will never perish in misery!

Yours, Anne

RUDYARD KIPLING

Brave men and women (as well as cowardly men and women) are not born that way; they become that way through their acts. Here are the acts that make us not just grow up, but grow up well.

> *If you can keep your head when all about you*
> *Are losing theirs and blaming it on you;*
> *If you can trust yourself when all men doubt you,*
> *But make allowance for their doubting too;*
> *If you can wait and not be tired by waiting,*
> *Or, being lied about, don't deal in lies,*
> *Or, being hated, don't give way to hating,*
> *And yet don't look too good, nor talk too wise;*
>
> *If you can dream—and not make dreams your master;*
> *If you can think—and not make thoughts your aim;*

If you can meet with triumph and disaster
And treat those two impostors just the same;
If you can bear to hear the truth you've spoken
Twisted by knaves to make a trap for fools,
Or watch the things you gave your life to broken,
And stoop and build 'em up with worn-out tools;

If you can make one heap of all your winnings
And risk it on one turn of pitch-and-toss,
And lose, and start again at your beginnings
And never breathe a word about your loss;
If you can force your heart and nerve and sinew
To serve your turn long after they are gone,
And so hold on when there is nothing in you
Except the Will which says to them: "Hold on!"

If you can talk with crowds and keep your virtue,
Or walk with kings—nor lose the common touch;
If neither foes nor loving friends can hurt you;
If all men count with you, but none too much;
If you can fill the unforgiving minute
With sixty seconds' worth of distance run—
Yours is the Earth and everything that's in it,
And—which is more—you'll be a Man, my son!

It Can Be Done

Courageous people think things through and ask: "Is this the best way to do this?" Cowards, on the other hand, always say, "It can't be done."

The man who misses all the fun
Is he who says, "It can't be done."
In solemn pride he stands aloof
And greets each venture with reproof.
Had he the power he'd efface
The history of the human race;
We'd have no radio or motor cars,
No streets lit by electric stars;
No telegraph nor telephone,
We'd linger in the age of stone.
The world would sleep if things were run
By men who say, "It can't be done."

Our Heroes

PHOEBE CARY

Seeing what is right and doing it with confidence is the mark of moral courage. Going against the crowd when the

crowd is wrong is something most courageous people must do
more than once in their lives.

> Here's a hand to the boy who has courage
> To do what he knows to be right;
> When he falls in the way of temptation,
> He has a hard battle to fight.
> Who strives against self and his comrades
> Will find a most powerful foe.
> All honor to him if he conquers.
> A cheer for the boy who says "NO!"

> There's many a battle fought daily
> The world knows nothing about;
> There's many a brave little soldier
> Whose strength puts a legion to rout.
> And he who fights sin singlehanded
> Is more of a hero, I say,
> Than he who leads soldiers to battle
> And conquers by arms in the fray.

> Be steadfast, my boy, when you're tempted,
> To do what you know to be right.
> Stand firm by the colors of manhood,
> And you will o'ercome in the fight.
> "The right," be your battle cry ever
> In waging the warfare of life,

And God, who knows who are the heroes,
Will give you the strength for the strife.

Rosa Parks
KAI FRIESE

When Rosa Parks refused to give up her seat on a bus, it led
to one of the most important chapters in the story of civil
rights in America. Parks's courage led to profound change
for African Americans.

It was Thursday, December 1, 1955. The workday was over,
and crowds of people boarded the green-and-white buses that
trundled through the streets of Montgomery. Rosa Parks was
tired after a full day of stitching and ironing shirts at the Montgomery Fair department store. She thought she was lucky to have
gotten one of the last seats in the rear section of the Cleveland
Avenue bus that would take her home.

Soon the back of the bus was full, and several people were
standing in the rear. The bus rolled on through Court Square,
where African Americans had been auctioned off during the days
of the Confederacy, and came to a stop in front of the Empire
Theater. The next passenger aboard stood in the front of an aisle.
He was a white man.

When he noticed that a white person had to stand, the bus

driver, James F. Blake, called out to the four black people who were sitting just behind the white section. He said they would have to give up their seats for the new passenger. No one stood up. "You'd better make it light on yourself and let me have those seats," the driver said threateningly. Three men got up and went to stand at the back of the bus. But Rosa Parks wasn't about to move. She had been in this situation before, and she had always given up her seat. She had always felt insulted by the experience. "It meant that I didn't have a right to do anything but get on the bus, give them my fare, and then be pushed around wherever they wanted me," she said.

By a quirk of fate, the driver of the bus on this December evening was the same James F. Blake who had once before removed the troublesome Rosa Parks from his bus for refusing to enter by the back door. That was a long time ago, in 1943. Rosa Parks didn't feel like being pushed around again. She told the driver that she wasn't in the white section and she wasn't going to move.

Blake knew the rules, though. He knew that the white section was wherever the driver said it was. If more white passengers got on the bus, he could stretch the white section to the back of the bus and make all the blacks stand. He shouted to Rosa Parks to move to the back of the bus. She wasn't impressed. She told him again that she wasn't moving. Everyone in the bus was silent, wondering what would happen next. Finally Blake told Rosa Parks that he would have her arrested for violating the racial segregation codes. In a firm but quiet voice, she told him that he could do what he wanted to do because she wasn't moving.

Blake got off the bus and came back with an officer of the Montgomery Police Department. As the officer placed Rosa Parks under arrest, she asked him plainly, "Why do you people push us around?"

With the eyes of all the passengers on him, the officer could only answer in confusion. "I don't know. I'm just obeying the law," he said.

Rosa Parks was taken to the police station, where she was booked and fingerprinted. While the policemen were filling out forms, she asked if she could have a drink of water. She was told that the drinking fountain in the station was for whites only. Then a policewoman marched her into a long corridor facing a wall of iron bars. A barred door slid open. She went inside. The door clanged shut, and she was locked in. She was in jail.

Rosa Parks's decision to challenge her arrest in court led Montgomery's black community to organize a bus boycott as a show of support.

Rosa Parks woke up on the morning of Monday, December 5, thinking about her trial. As she and her husband got out of bed, they heard the familiar sound of a City Lines bus pulling up to a stop across the road. There was usually a crowd of people waiting for the bus at this time. The Parkses rushed to the window and looked out. Except for the driver, the bus was empty and there was no one getting on either. The bus stood at the stop for more than a minute, puffing exhaust smoke into the cold December air as the puzzled driver waited for passengers. But no one appeared, and the empty bus chugged away.

Rosa Parks was filled with happiness. Her neighbors were actually boycotting the buses. She couldn't wait to drive to the courthouse so that she could see how the boycott was going in the rest of Montgomery. When Fred Gray arrived to drive her to the trial, she wasn't disappointed. Rosa Parks had expected some people to stay off the buses. She thought that with luck, maybe even half the usual passengers would stay off. But these buses were just plain empty.

All over the city, empty buses bounced around for everyone to see. There was never more than the usual small group of white passengers in front and sometimes a lonely black passenger in back, wondering what was going on. The streets were filled with black people walking to work.

As Rosa Parks and her lawyer drove up to the courthouse, there was another surprise waiting for them. A crowd of about five hundred blacks had gathered to show their support for her. Mrs. Parks and the lawyer made their way slowly through the cheering crowd into the courtroom. Once they were inside, the trial didn't take long. Rosa Parks was quickly convicted of breaking the bus segregation laws and fined ten dollars, as well as four dollars for the cost of her trial. This was the stage at which Claudette Colvin's trial had ended seven months earlier. Colvin had had little choice but to accept the guilty verdict and pay the fine.

This time, however, Fred Gray rose to file an appeal on Rosa

Parks's case. This meant that her case would be taken to a higher court at a later date. Meanwhile, Mrs. Parks was free to go.

Outside the courthouse, the crowd was getting restless. Some of them were carrying sawed-off shotguns, and the policemen were beginning to look worried. E. D. Nixon went out to calm them, but nobody could hear him in the din. Voices from the crowd shouted out that they would storm the courthouse if Rosa Parks didn't come out safely within a few minutes. When she did appear, a great cheer went up again.

After seeing the empty buses that morning, and this large and fearless crowd around her now, Rosa Parks knew that she had made the right decision. Black people were uniting to show the city administration that they were tired of the insults of segregation. Together, they could change Montgomery. They could do some good.

Susan B. Anthony
JOANNA STRONG AND TOM B. LEONARD

The Nineteenth Amendment to the Constitution, which provides for full woman suffrage, was not ratified until fourteen years after Susan B. Anthony's death in 1906. Nevertheless, her name more than any other is associated with American women's long struggle to vote. Her firm resolve made her one of our greatest examples of political courage.

"What the blazes are you doing here?" shouted the man at the big desk. "You women go home about your business. Go home and wash the dishes. And if you don't clear out of here fast, I'll get the cops to put you out!"

Everybody in the store stopped and listened. Some of the men just turned around and sneered. Others looked at the fifteen women mockingly and guffawed. One man piped, "Beat it, youse dames. Your kids are dirty." And at that, every man in the place bellowed with laughter.

But this banter didn't faze the tall, dignified woman who stood with a piece of paper in her hand at the head of the fourteen other ladies. She didn't budge an inch.

"I've come here to vote for the President of the United States," she said. "He will be my President as well as yours. We are the women who bear the children who will defend this country. We are the women who make your homes, who bake your bread, who rear your sons and give you daughters. We women are citizens of this country just as much as you are, and we insist on voting for the man who is to be the leader of this government."

Her words rang out with the clearness of a bell, and they struck to the heart. No man in the place dared move now. The big man at the desk who had threatened her was turned to stone. And then, in silence and dignity, Susan B. Anthony strode up to the ballot box and dropped into it the paper bearing her vote. Each of the other fourteen women did the same, while every man in the room stood silent and watched.

It was the year 1872. Too long now had women been denied

the rights that should naturally be theirs. Too long now had they endured the injustice of an unfair law—a law that made them mere possessions of men.

Women could earn money, but they might not own it. If a woman was married and went to work, every penny she earned became the property of her husband. In 1872, a man was considered complete master of the household. His wife was taken to be incapable of managing her own affairs. She was supposed to be a nitwit unable to think clearly, and therefore the law mercifully protected her by appointing a guardian—a male guardian, of course—over any property that she was lucky enough to possess.

Women like Susan Anthony writhed at this injustice. Susan saw no reason why her sex should be discriminated against. "Why should only men make the laws?" she cried. "Why should men forge the chains that bind us down? No!" she exclaimed. "It is up to us women to fight for our rights." And then she vowed that she would carry on an everlasting battle, as long as the Lord gave her strength to see that women were made equal in the sight of the law.

And fight she did. Susan B. Anthony was America's greatest champion of women's rights. She traveled unceasingly, from one end of the country to the other. She made thousands of speeches, pleading with men, and trying to arouse women to fight for their rights. She wrote hundreds of pamphlets and letters of protest. It was a bitter and difficult struggle that she entered upon, for the people who opposed her did not hesitate to say all kinds of ugly and untrue things about her and her followers. "No decent woman would talk like that. No refined lady would force her way before judges and men's associations and insist on talking. She is vulgar!"

Many women who knew that Susan Anthony was a refined, intelligent, and courageous woman were afraid to say so. They were afraid that *they* would be looked down on. But in time, they grew to love her for trying to help them.

After a while, many housewives gained courage from her example. Then, in great meetings, they joined her by the thousands. Many a man began to change his notions when his wife, inspired by Susan B. Anthony, made him feel ashamed at the unfair treatment accorded women. Slowly the great Susan B. Anthony was undermining the fierce stubbornness of men.

On that important day in 1872, she and her faithful followers cast their first ballots for President. But though the men in the polling place were momentarily moved, their minds were not yet opened. In a few days, Susan was arrested and brought before a judge, accused of having illegally entered a voting booth.

"How do you plead?" asked the judge.

"Guilty!" cried Susan. "Guilty of trying to uproot the slavery in which you men have placed us women. Guilty of trying to make you see that we mothers are as important to this country as are the men. Guilty of trying to lift the standard of womanhood, so that men may look with pride upon their wives' awareness of public affairs."

And then, before the judge could recover from this onslaught, she added, "But, Your Honor, *not* guilty of acting against the Constitution of the United States, which says that no person is to be deprived of equal rights under the law. Equal rights!" she thundered. "How can it be said that we women have equal rights, when it is you and you alone who take upon yourselves the right to make the laws, the right to choose your representatives, the right to send only sons to higher education. You, you blind men, have become slaveholders of your own mothers and wives."

The judge was taken aback. Never before had he heard these ideas expressed to him in such a forceful manner. However, the law was the law! The judge spoke quietly, and without much conviction. "I am forced to fine you one hundred dollars," he said.

"I will not pay it!" said Susan Anthony. "Mark my words, the law will be changed!" And with that, she strode from the court.

"Shall I follow her and bring her back?" said the court clerk to the judge. "No, let her go," answered the elderly judge. "I fear that she is right, and that the law will soon be changed."

And Susan did go on, on to further crusades, on across the vast stretches of the United States, proclaiming in every hamlet where her feet trod, her plea for womanhood.

Today, voting by women is an established fact. Women may keep what they earn; and whether married or single, own their own property. It is taken for granted that a woman may go to college and work in any business or profession she may choose. But these rights, enjoyed by the women of today, were secured through the valiant effort of many fighters for women's freedom, such as the great Susan B. Anthony.

The Leopard's Revenge

Courage involves knowing what to fear, but that in itself is not enough, as this African folktale reminds us. The father leopard of this story may be smart to know his limits, but his taking revenge on a weaker, innocent party is hardly courageous.

Once a leopard cub strayed from his home and ventured into the midst of a great herd of elephants. His mother and father had warned him to stay out of the way of the giant beasts, but he did not listen. Suddenly, the elephants began to stampede, and one of them stepped on the cub without even knowing it. Soon afterward, a hyena found his body and went to tell his parents.

"I have terrible news," he said. "I've found your son lying dead in the field."

The mother and father leopard gave great cries of grief and rage.

"How did it happen?" the father demanded. "Tell me who did this to our son! I will never rest until I have my revenge!"

"The elephants did it," answered the hyena.

"The elephants?" asked the father leopard, quite startled. "You say it was the elephants?"

"Yes," said the hyena, "I saw their tracks."

The leopard paced back and forth for a few minutes, growling and shaking his head.

"No, you are wrong," he said at last. "It was not the elephants. It was the goats. The goats have murdered my boy!"

And at once he bounded down the hill and sprang upon a herd of goats grazing in the valley below, and in a violent rage killed as many as he could in revenge.

The Minotaur

ADAPTED FROM ANDREW LANG

This Greek myth is a story of compassion and courage. There are two heroes here: The first is Theseus, who goes into the maze to save his countrymen. The second is Ariadne, who searches her heart and realizes she must defy her own father to save Theseus and the others. We can be sure that both Theseus and Ariadne were afraid of the danger they faced, but they did the right thing anyway. It is not the absence of fear that defines courage, but doing the right thing despite one's fears.

This story begins in Athens, one of the greatest and most noble cities of ancient Greece. At the time it takes place, however, Athens was only a little town, perched on the top of a cliff rising out of the plain, two or three miles from the sea. King Aegeus, who ruled Athens in those days, had just welcomed home a son he had not seen since the child's birth, a youth named Theseus, who was destined to become one of Greece's greatest heroes.

Aegeus was overjoyed at having his son home at last, but Theseus could not help but notice moments when the king seemed
distracted and sad. Gradually, Theseus began to sense the same
melancholy among the people of Athens. Mothers were silent,
fathers shook their heads, and young people watched the sea all
day, as if they expected something fearful to come from it. Many
of the Athenian youth seemed to be missing, and were said to
have gone to visit friends in faraway parts of Greece. At last Theseus decided to ask his father what troubled the land.

"I'm afraid you've come home at an unhappy time," Aegeus
sighed. "There is a curse upon Athens, a curse so terrible and
strange that not even you, Prince Theseus, can deal with it."

"Tell me all," said Theseus, "for though I am but one man, yet
the ever-living gods protect me and help me."

"The trouble is an old one," Aegeus said. "It dates to a time
when young men came to Athens from all over Greece and other
lands to take part in contests in running, boxing, wrestling, and
foot races. The son of the great Minos, king of Crete, was among
the contestants, and he died while he was here. His death is still
a puzzle to me. Some say it was an accident; others say he was
murdered by jealous rivals. At any rate, his comrades fled in the
night, bearing the news to Crete.

"The sea was black with King Minos's ships when he arrived
seeking vengeance. His army was far too powerful for us. We
went humbly out of the city to meet him and ask for mercy.
'This is the mercy I will show you,' he said. 'I will not burn
your city, I will not take your treasures, and I will not make

your people my captives. But every seven years, you must pay a tribute. You must swear to choose by lot seven youths and seven maidens, and send them to me.' We had no choice but to agree. Every seven years, a ship with black sails arrives from Crete and bears away the captives. This is the seventh year, and the coming of the ship is at hand."

"And what happens to them once they reach Crete?" Theseus asked.

"We do not know, because they never return. But the sailors of Minos say he places them in a strange prison, a kind of maze, called the Labyrinth. It is full of dark winding ways, cut in the solid rock, and therein lives a horrible monster called the Minotaur. This monster has the body of a man, but his head is the head of a bull, and his teeth are the teeth of a lion, and he devours everyone he meets. That, I fear, is the fate of our Athenian youth."

"We could burn the black-sailed ship when it arrives, and slay its sailors," Theseus said.

"Yes, we could," answered Aegeus, "but then Minos would return with his fleet and his army, and destroy all of Athens."

"Then let me go as one of the captives," said Theseus, rising to his feet, "and I will slay the Minotaur. I am your son and heir, and it is only right that I try to free Athens of this awful curse."

Aegeus tried to persuade his son that such a plan was useless, but Theseus was determined, and when the ship with black sails touched the shore, he joined the doomed group. His father came to tell him goodbye for the last time, weeping bitterly.

"If you do manage to come back alive," he said to Theseus, "lower the black sails as you approach, and hoist white sails in their place, so that I may know you did not die in the Labyrinth."

"Do not worry," Theseus told him. "Look for white sails. I will return in triumph." As he spoke, the dark ship put to sea and soon sailed past the horizon.

After many days' sailing, the ship reached Crete. The Athenian prisoners were marched to the palace, where King Minos sat on his gilded throne, surrounded by his chiefs and princes, all gloriously clothed in silken robes and jewels of gold. Minos, a dark-faced man with touches of white in his hair and long beard, sat with his elbow on his knee and his chin in his hand, and he fixed his eyes on the eyes of Theseus. Theseus bowed and then stood erect, with his eyes on the eyes of Minos.

"You are fifteen in number," Minos said at last, "and my law claims only fourteen."

"I came of my own will," answered Theseus.

"Why?" asked Minos.

"The people of Athens have a mind to be free, O King."

"There is a way," said Minos. "Slay the Minotaur, and you are free of my tribute."

"I am minded to slay him," said Theseus, and as he spoke, there was a stir in the throng of chiefs and princes, and a beautiful young woman glided through them and stood a little behind the throne. This was Ariadne, the daughter of Minos, a wise and tender-hearted maiden. Theseus bowed low, and again stood erect, with his eyes on the face of Ariadne.

"You speak like a king's son," Minos said with a smile. "Perhaps one who has never known hardship."

"I have known hardship, and my name is Theseus, Aegeus's son. I have come to ask you to let me face the Minotaur alone. If I cannot slay it, my companions will follow me into the Labyrinth."

"I see," Minos said. "Very well. The king's son wishes to die alone. Let him do so."

The Athenians were led upstairs and along galleries, each to a chamber more rich and beautiful than they had seen before in their dreams. Each was taken to a bath, and washed and clothed in new garments, and then treated to a lavish feast. None had the appetite to eat, though, except Theseus, who knew he would need his strength.

That night as he was preparing for bed, Theseus heard a soft knock at his door, and suddenly Ariadne, the king's daughter, was standing in his room. Once again Theseus gazed into her eyes and saw there was a kind of strength and compassion he had never known before.

"Too many of your countrymen have disappeared into my father's Labyrinth," she said quietly. "I have brought you a dagger, and I can show you and your friends the way to flee."

"I thank you for the dagger," Theseus answered, "but I cannot flee. If you wish to show me a way, show me the way to the Minotaur."

"Even if you are strong enough to kill the monster," Ariadne whispered, "you will need to find your way out of the Labyrinth. It is made of so many dark twists and turns, so many dead ends and false passages, not even my father knows the secrets of its windings. If you are determined to go forward with your plan, you must take this with you." She took from her gown a spool of gold thread, and pressed it into Theseus's hand.

"As soon as you get inside the Labyrinth," she said, "tie the end of the thread to a stone, and hold tight to the spool as you wander through the maze. When you are ready to come back, the thread will be your guide."

Theseus gazed at her, hardly knowing what to say. "Why are you doing this?" he finally asked. "If your father finds out, you'll be in great danger."

"Yes," Ariadne answered slowly, "but if I had not acted, you and your friends would be in far greater danger."

And Theseus knew then that he loved her.

The next morning Theseus was led to the Labyrinth. As soon as the guards shut him inside, he fastened one end of the thread to a pointed rock, and began to walk slowly, keeping firm hold of the precious string. He made his way down the broadest corridor, from which others turned off to the right and left, until he came to a wall. He retraced his steps, and tried another hallway, and then another, always stopping every few feet to listen for the monster. He passed through many dark, winding passages, sometimes coming to places he had already been before, but gradually descending further and further into the Labyrinth. Finally he reached a room heaped high with bones, and he knew now he was very near the beast.

He sat still, and from far away he heard a faint sound, like the end of the echo of a roar. He stood up and listened keenly. The sound came nearer and louder, not deep like the roar of a bull, but more shrill and thin. Theseus stooped quickly and scooped up a handful of dirt from the floor of the Labyrinth, and with his other hand drew his dagger.

The roars of the Minotaur came nearer and nearer. Now his feet could be heard thudding along the echoing floor. There was a heavy rustling, then sniffing, then silence. Theseus moved to the shadowy corner of the narrow path and crouched there. His heart was beating quickly. On came the Minotaur—it caught sight of the crouching figure, gave a great roar, and rushed straight for it. Theseus leaped up and, dodging to one side, dashed his handful of dirt into the beast's eyes.

The Minotaur bellowed in pain. It rubbed its eyes with its monstrous hands, shrieking and confused. It tossed its great head up and down, and it turned around and around, feeling with its hands for the wall. It was quite blind. Theseus drew his dagger, crept up behind the monster, and quickly slashed at its legs. Down fell the Minotaur, with a crash and a roar, biting at the rocky floor with its lion's teeth, waving its hands, and clawing at the empty air. Theseus waited for his chance, when the clutching hands rested, and then three times he drove the sharp blade through the heart of the Minotaur. The body leaped and lay still.

Theseus kneeled and thanked all the gods, and when he had finished his prayer, he took his dagger and hacked off the head of the Minotaur. With the head in his hand, he began following the string out of the Labyrinth. It seemed he would never come out of those dark, gloomy passages. Had the thread snapped some-where, and had he, after all, lost his way? But still he followed it anxiously, until at last he came to the entrance, and he sank to the ground, worn out with his struggle and his wanderings.

"I don't know what miracle caused you to come out of the Labyrinth alive," Minos said when he saw the monster's head, "but I will keep my word. I promised you freedom if you slew the Minotaur. You and your comrades may go. Now let there be peace between your people and mine. Farewell."

Theseus knew he owed his life and his country's freedom to Ariadne's courage, and he knew he could not leave without her. Some say he asked Minos for her hand in marriage, and that the king gladly consented. Others say she stole onto the departing ship at the last minute without her father's knowledge. Either way, the two lovers were together when the anchor lifted and the dark ship sailed away from Crete.

But this happy ending is mixed with tragedy, as stories some-times are. For the Cretan captain of the vessel did not know he was to hoist white sails if Theseus came home in triumph, and King Aegeus, as he anxiously watched the waters from a high cliff, spied the black sails coming over the horizon. His heart broke at once, and he fell from the towering cliff into the sea, which is now called the Aegean.

HONESTY

Honesty

When you think of someone's reputation, you usually think first of his or her honesty. If you say, "He's a man of honor," you mean that person is someone who tells the truth, keeps his word, and does what he says he's going to do. When you are deciding whether or not you want to associate with someone, his honesty is probably one of the first yardsticks you'll use to measure him.

George Washington wrote, "I hope I shall always possess firmness and virtue enough to maintain what I consider the most enviable of all titles, the character of an honest man." He knew that honesty is usually a good reputation's greatest possession, as well as its greatest armor for staying good. Whatever other good traits someone possesses, they do a reputation no good without honesty. Someone may be smart, friendly, hard-working, and determined, but all those qualities are poisoned by deceit.

Very early on, you will be identified by classmates and friends as an honest or dishonest person. When people know you are honest they will like you, rely on you, and want to be around you. Here, however, is the sober truth about dishonest reputations: No one wants to be around a liar. So it is very important that you guard your honest reputation. Just one or two lies can destroy it very quickly. A reputation for not telling the truth, on the other hand, may take a very long time to erase.

You guard your honest reputation by constantly practicing honesty. Like any other habit, honesty must be cultivated. The more you do it, the more it becomes a part of your nature.

Lying, like any other bad habit, usually starts in small, seemingly harmless measures. "He who permits himself to tell a lie once," Thomas Jefferson wrote, "finds it much easier to do it a second time, till at length it becomes habitual. He tells lies without attending to it, and truths without the world's believing him. This falsehood of the tongue leads to that of the heart, and in time depraves all its good dispositions." So we have to guard against "little white lies" that eventually may destroy our love of the truth.

Sometimes honesty has its costs. A friend may want you to do something wrong, and you may make him angry—even lose the friendship—by saying no. Or you may have to watch others get ahead by cheating or playing loose with the rules. At times like that, you may be tempted to think that perhaps crime does pay. And occasionally it does—but only for a short while. Eventually, dishonesty catches up with those who practice it. In the meantime, it's best to remember the words of Sir Thomas More in Robert Bolt's play, *A Man For All Seasons:* "Since in fact we see that avarice, anger, envy, pride, sloth, lust, and stupidity commonly profit far beyond humility, chastity, fortitude, justice, and thought, and have to choose, to be human at all . . . then perhaps we *must* stand fast a little—even at the risk of being heroes."

In the end, honesty is more than telling the truth to other people. It also means being honest with ourselves. It means doing the right thing even when we know no one else is looking. Why? One reason is that deceit takes a terrible toll on our own sense of self-respect. It can make us nothing but unhappy. Another reason was stated by the ancient Greek philosopher Demosthenes, who pointed out that "what we have in us of the image of God is the love of truth."

Honest Abe

RETOLD BY HORATIO ALGER

Our two most beloved American presidents, Washington and Lincoln, are remembered for their honesty. The following tales remind us that honesty in private life makes honesty in public office. More important, they show us that habits of a truthful heart begin early in life.

THE YOUNG STOREKEEPER

As a clerk, Abe proved honest and efficient, and my readers will be interested in some illustrations of the former trait which I find in Dr. Holland's interesting volume.

One day a woman came into the store and purchased sundry articles. They footed up two dollars and six and a quarter cents, or the young clerk thought they did. We do not hear nowadays of six and a quarter cents, but this was a coin borrowed from the Spanish currency, and was well known in my own boyhood.

The bill was paid, and the woman was entirely satisfied. But the young storekeeper, not feeling quite sure as to the accuracy of his calculation, added up the items once more. To his dismay he found that the sum total should have been but two dollars.

"I've made her pay six and a quarter cents too much," said Abe, disturbed.

It was a trifle, and many clerks would have dismissed it as such. But Abe was too conscientious for that.

"The money must be paid back," he decided.

This would have been easy enough had the woman lived "just round the corner," but, as the young man knew, she lived between two and three miles away. This, however, did not alter the matter. It was night, but he closed and locked the store, and walked to the residence of his customer. Arrived there, he explained the matter, paid over the six and a quarter cents, and returned satisfied. If I were a capitalist, I would be willing to lend money to such a young man without security.

Here is another illustration of young Lincoln's strict honesty:

A woman entered the store and asked for half a pound of tea.

The young clerk weighed it out and handed it to her in a parcel. This was the last sale of the day.

The next morning, when commencing his duties, Abe discovered a four-ounce weight on the scales. It flashed upon him at once that he had used this in the sale of the night previous, and so, of course, given his customer short weight. I am afraid that there are many country merchants who would not have been much worried by this discovery. Not so the young clerk in whom we are interested. He weighed out the balance of the half pound, shut up the store, and carried it to the defrauded customer. I think my young readers will begin to see that the name so often given, in later times to President Lincoln, of "Honest Old Abe," was well deserved. A man who begins by strict honesty in his youth is not likely to change as he grows older, and mercantile honesty is some guarantee of political honesty.

WORKING OUT A BOOK

All the information we can obtain about this early time is interesting for it was then that Abe was laying the foundation of his future eminence. His mind and character were slowly developing, and shaping themselves for the future.

From Mr. Lamon's *Life* I quote a paragraph which will throw light upon his habits and tastes at the age of seventeen:

"Abe loved to lie under a shade tree, or up in the loft of the cabin, and read, cipher, and scribble. At night he sat by the chimney jamb, and ciphered by the light of the fire, on the wooden fire shovel. When the shovel was fairly covered, he would shave it off with Tom Lincoln's drawing knife, and begin again. In the daytime he used boards for the same purpose, out of doors, and went through the shaving process everlastingly. His stepmother repeats often that 'he read every book he could lay his hands on.' She says, 'Abe read diligently. He read every book he could lay his hands on, and when he came across a passage that struck him, he would write it down on boards if he had no paper, and keep it there until he did get paper. Then he would rewrite it, look at it, repeat it. He had a copybook, a kind of scrapbook, in which he put down all things, and thus preserved them.'"

I am tempted also to quote a reminiscence of John Hanks, who lived with the Lincolns from the time Abe was fourteen to the time he became eighteen years of age: "When Lincoln—Abe—and I returned to the house from work, he would go to the cupboard, snatch a piece of cornbread, take down a book, sit down on a chair, cock his legs up as high as his head, and read.

He and I worked barefooted, grubbed it, plowed, mowed, and cradled together; plowed corn, gathered it, and shucked corn. Abraham read constantly when he had opportunity."

It may well be supposed, however, that the books upon which Abe could lay hands were few in number. There were no libraries, either public or private, in the neighborhood, and he was obliged to read what he could get rather than those which he would have chosen, had he been able to select from a large collection. Still, it is a matter of interest to know what books he actually did read at this formative period. Some of them certainly were worth reading, such as *Aesop's Fables, Robinson Crusoe, Pilgrim's Progress, a History of the United States,* and Weems's *Life of Washington.* The last book Abe borrowed from a neighbor, old Josiah Crawford (I follow the statement of Mr. Lamon, rather than of Dr. Holland, who says it was Master Crawford, his teacher). When not reading it, he laid it away in a part of the cabin where he thought it would be free from harm, but it so happened that just behind the shelf on which he placed it was a great crack between the logs of the wall. One night a storm came up suddenly, the rain beat in through the crevice, and soaked the borrowed book through and through. The book was almost utterly spoiled. Abe felt very uneasy, for a book was valuable in his eyes, as well as in the eyes of its owner.

He took the damaged volume and trudged over to Mr. Crawford's in some perplexity and mortification.

"Well, Abe, what brings you over so early?" said Mr. Crawford.

"I've got some bad news for you," answered Abe, with lengthened face.

"Bad news! What is it?"

"You know the book you lent me—*The Life of Washington?*"

"Yes, yes."

"Well, the rain last night spoiled it." And Abe showed the book, wet to a pulp inside, at the same time explaining how it had been injured.

"It's too bad, I vum! You'd ought to pay for it, Abe. You must have been dreadful careless!"

"I'd pay for it if I had any money, Mr. Crawford."

"If you've got no money, you can work it out," said Crawford.

"I'll do whatever you think right."

So it was arranged that Abe should work three days for Crawford, "pulling fodder," the value of his labor being rated at twenty-five cents a day. As the book had cost seventy-five cents this would be regarded as satisfactory. So Abe worked his three days, and discharged the debt. Mr. Lamon is disposed to find fault with Crawford for exacting this penalty, but it appears to me only equitable, and I am glad to think that Abe was willing to act honorably in the matter.

The Character of a Happy Life
HENRY WOTTEN

Honesty is armor for the soul.

> *How happy is he born and taught,*
> *That serveth not another's will;*

Whose armor is his honest thought,
And simple truth his utmost skill!
Whose passions not his masters are,
Whose soul is still prepared for death,
Untied unto the worldly care
Of public fame, or private breath;

Who envies none that chance doth raise,
Or vice; who never understood
How deepest wounds are given by praise;
Nor rules of state, but rules of good:

Who hath his life from rumors freed,
Whose conscience is his strong retreat;
Whose state can neither flatterers feed,
Nor ruin make oppressors great;

Who God doth late and early pray,
More of his grace than gifts to lend;
And entertains the harmless day
With a religious book or friend.

This man is freed from servile bands,
Or hope to rise, or fear to fall;
Lord of himself, though not of lands;
And having nothing, yet hath all.

The Emperor and the Peasant Boy

*This old tale from Mexico reminds us that one heart's honesty
has the power to turn others in the right direction.*

Long ago, during the days of the Aztec empire in what we
now call Mexico, there ruled an emperor who sometimes liked
to disguise himself and walk the city streets and country foot-
paths alone. He knew his subjects would speak far more openly
and fearlessly to a common stranger than to their own emperor,
and he was able to learn much about his people he would not
have known had he always stayed on his throne.

One day the disguised emperor was wandering the coun-
tryside when he came upon a little peasant boy gathering a few
sticks of firewood so his family might cook their dinner.

"You are working hard, my little friend," the emperor said,
"but there's barely enough wood here to start a fire. Why don't
you go into that thick forest on the hillside? There are plenty of
sticks to be picked up there."

The boy shook his head.

"That hillside is part of the emperor's forest. He has set it
aside for his hunting parties. No one may enter without his permission, and to pick up sticks there would mean instant death."

"Only if you were caught." The emperor smiled. "The forest
is deserted now, and you could slip in and out easily. No one will
see you, and I promise I will keep quiet."

"Thanks for the advice," the boy replied coldly, "but I think I'll just gather what I find here."

"But think of all that wood going to waste on the forest floor! Surely your emperor must be a selfish, unkind ruler not to share it with you."

"It's true this law is harsh and unfair," the boy said angrily. "The emperor has no use for the sticks in the forest, and yet he denies them to many in need. But should I do wrong because the law is unjust? No, I will not enter the forest, not as long as there is a better way."

The boy picked up his meager bundle of sticks and turned for home with tears in his eyes.

The next day a royal messenger appeared at the peasant boy's home and commanded his whole family to come to the palace at once. They set out in fear and trembling, unable to imagine why they were being summoned.

They were led before the emperor himself, sitting on his throne in all his royal garb. The peasant boy recognized his face at once, and he paled with terror.

"You were the one who urged me to enter the royal forest!" he cried.

"Don't be afraid," the emperor said. "You've done no wrong. You refused to steal when you had the chance, and you insisted on obeying your emperor's law. I want to meet your parents. They have raised you well, and will be rewarded."

He pointed to a chest of gold, enough to keep want from their humble door for the rest of their lives.

"But there is something more important," the emperor went on. "You were right about my law. It is unjust. From now on, the royal forest is open to all."

He took the peasant boy by the arm.

"You wondered if there were not a better way," he said. "There was. Your virtue has reached the heart of your emperor."

The Good Bishop
ADAPTED FROM VICTOR HUGO

In this story from Victor Hugo's Les Miserables, *we see a lie told to help another. This is one of those rare occasions when lying makes sense.*

Jean Valjean was a wood-chopper's son, who, while very young, was left an orphan. His older sister brought him up, but when he was seventeen years of age, his sister's husband died, and upon Jean came the labor of supporting her seven little children. Although a man of great strength, he found it very difficult to provide food for them at the poor trade he followed.

One winter day he was without work, and the children were crying for bread. They were nearly starved. And, when he could withstand their entreaties no longer, he went out in the night, and, breaking a baker's window with his fist, carried home a loaf of bread for the famished children. The next morning he was arrested for stealing, his bleeding hand convicting him.

For this crime he was sent to the galleys with an iron collar riveted around his neck, with a chain attached, which bound him to his galley seat. Here he remained four years, then he tried to escape, but was caught, and three years were added to his sentence. Then he made a second attempt, and also failed, the result of which was that he remained nineteen years as a galley slave for stealing a single loaf of bread.

When Jean left the prison, his heart was hardened. He felt like a wolf. His wrongs had embittered him, and he was more like an animal than a man. He came with every man's hand raised against him to the town where the good bishop lived.

At the inn they would not receive him because they knew him to be an ex-convict and a dangerous man. Wherever he went, the knowledge of him went before, and everyone drove him away. They would not even allow him to sleep in a dog kennel or give him the food they had saved for the dog. Everywhere he went they cried: "Be off! Go away, or you will get a charge of shot." Finally, he wandered to the house of the good bishop, and a good man he was.

For his duties as a bishop, he received from the state 3,000 francs a year; but he gave away to the poor 2,800 francs of it. He was a simple, loving man, with a great heart, who thought nothing of himself, but loved everybody. And everybody loved him.

Jean, when he entered the bishop's house, was a most forbidding and dangerous character. He shouted in a harsh loud voice:

"Look here, I am a galley slave. Here is my yellow passport. It says: 'Five years for robbery and fourteen years for trying to escape. The man is very dangerous.' Now that you know who I am, will you give me a little food, and let me sleep in the stable?"

The good bishop said: "Sit down and warm yourself. You will take supper with me, and after that sleep here."

Jean could hardly believe his senses. He was dumb with joy. He told the bishop that he had money, and would pay for his supper and lodging.

But the priest said: "You are welcome. This is not my house, but the house of Christ. Your name was known to me before you showed me your passport. You are my brother."

After supper the bishop took one of the silver candlesticks that he had received as a Christmas present, and, giving Jean the other, led him to his room, where a good bed was provided. In the middle of the night Jean awoke with a hardened heart. He felt that the time had come to get revenge for all his wrongs. He remembered the silver knives and forks that had been used for supper, and made up his mind to steal them, and go away in the night. So he took what he could find, sprang into the garden, and disappeared.

When the bishop awoke, and saw his silver gone, he said: "I have been thinking for a long time that I ought not to keep the silver. I should have given it to the poor, and certainly this man was poor."

At breakfast time five soldiers brought Jean back to the bishop's house. When they entered, the bishop, looking at him, said:

"Oh, you are back again! I am glad to see you. I gave you the candlesticks, too, which are silver also, and will bring forty francs. Why did you not take them?"

Jean was stunned indeed by these words. So were the soldiers. "This man told us the truth, did he?" they cried. "We thought he had stolen the silver and was running away. So we quickly arrested him."

But the good bishop only said: "It was a mistake to have him brought back. Let him go. The silver is his. I gave it to him."

So the officers went away.

"Is it true," Jean whispered to the bishop, "that I am free? I may go?"

"Yes," he replied, "but before you go take your candlesticks."

Jean trembled in every limb, and took the candlesticks like one in a dream.

"Now," said the bishop, "depart in peace, but do not go through the garden, for the front door is always open to you day and night."

Jean looked as though he would faint.

Then the bishop took his hand, and said: "Never forget you have promised me you would use the money to become an honest man."

He did not remember having promised anything, but stood silent while the bishop continued solemnly:

"Jean Valjean, my brother, you no longer belong to evil, but to good. I have bought your soul for you. I withdrew it from black thoughts and the spirit of hate, and gave it to God."

The Indian Cinderella

RETOLD BY CYRUS MACMILLAN

This North American Indian tale is about how honesty is rewarded and dishonesty punished. Glooskap, mentioned in the opening paragraph, was a god of the Eastern Woodlands Indians.

On the shores of a wide bay on the Atlantic coast there dwelt in old times a great Indian warrior. It was said that he had been one of Glooskap's best helpers and friends, and that he had done for him many wonderful deeds. But that, no man knows. He had, however, a very wonderful and strange power: He could make himself invisible. He could thus mingle unseen with his enemies and listen to their plots. He was known among the people as Strong Wind, the Invisible. He dwelt with his sister in a tent near the sea, and his sister helped him greatly in his work. Many maidens would have been glad to marry him, and he was much sought after because of his mighty deeds; and it was known that Strong Wind would marry the first maiden who could see him as he came home at night. Many made the trial, but it was a long time before one succeeded.

Strong Wind used a clever trick to test the truthfulness of all who sought to win him. Each evening as the day went down, his sister walked on the beach with any girl who wished to make the trial. His sister could always see him, but no one else could see him. And as he came home from work in the twilight, his sister as she saw him drawing near would ask the girl who sought him, "Do you see him?" And each girl would falsely answer "Yes." And his sister would ask, "With what does he draw his sled?" And each girl would answer, "With the hide of a moose," or "With a pole," or "With a great cord." And then his sister would know that they all had lied, for their answers were mere guesses. And many tried and lied and failed, for Strong Wind would not marry any who were untruthful.

There lived in the village a great chief who had three daughters. Their mother had long been dead. One of these was much younger than the others. She was very beautiful and gentle and well beloved by all, and for that reason her older sisters were very jealous of her charms and treated her very cruelly. They clothed her in rags that she might be ugly; and they cut off her long black hair; and they burned her face with coals from the fire that she might be scarred and disfigured. And they lied to their father, telling him that she had done these things herself. But the girl was patient and kept her gentle heart and went gladly about her work.

Like other girls, the chief's two eldest daughters tried to win Strong Wind. One evening, as the day went down, they walked on the shore with Strong Wind's sister and waited for his coming. Soon he came home from his day's work, drawing his sled. And his sister asked as usual, "Do you see him?" And each one, lying, answered "Yes." And she asked, "Of what is his shoulder strap made?" And each, guessing, said "Of rawhide." Then they entered the tent where they hoped to see Strong Wind eating his supper;

and when he took off his coat and his moccasins they could see them, but more than these they saw nothing. And Strong Wind knew that they had lied, and he kept himself from their sight, and they went home dismayed.

One day the chief's youngest daughter with her rags and her burned face resolved to seek Strong Wind. She patched her clothes with bits of birch bark from the trees, and put on the few little ornaments she possessed, and went forth to try to see the Invisible One as all the other girls of the village had done before. And her sisters laughed at her and called her "fool." And as she passed along the road all the people laughed at her because of her tattered frock and her burned face, but silently she went her way.

Strong Wind's sister received the little girl kindly, and at twilight she took her to the beach. Soon Strong Wind came home drawing his sled. And his sister asked, "Do you see him?" And the girl answered "No," and his sister wondered greatly because she spoke the truth. And again she asked, "Do you see him now?" And the girl answered, "Yes, and he is very wonderful." And she asked, "With what does he draw his sled?" And the girl answered, "With the Rainbow," and she was much afraid. And she asked further, "Of what is his bowstring?" And the girl answered, "His bowstring is the Milky Way."

Then Strong Wind's sister knew that because the girl had spoken the truth at first her brother had made himself visible to her. And she said, "Truly, you have seen him." And she took her home and bathed her, and all the scars disappeared from her face and body; and her hair grew long and black again like the raven's wing; and she gave her fine clothes to wear and many rich orna-ments. Then she bade her take the wife's seat in the tent. Soon Strong Wind entered and sat beside her, and called her his bride. The very next day she became his wife, and ever afterward she helped him to do great deeds. The girl's two elder sisters were very cross and they wondered greatly at what had taken place. But Strong Wind, who knew of their cruelty, resolved to punish them. Using his great power, he changed them both into aspen trees and rooted them in the earth. And since that day the leaves of the aspen have always trembled, and they shiver in fear at the approach of Strong Wind, it matters not how softly he comes, for they are still mindful of his great power and anger because of their lies and their cruelty to their sister long ago.

The Lie That Deserved Another

Exaggerations seldom go unnoticed, as this tale from Southeast Asia shows us.

A man returned home after traveling abroad, eager to brag about his adventures.

"I've seen things you've never imagined, not even in your dreams," he told his friends. "Once I saw the longest ship afloat. The captain was standing at the stern, and he gave the cabin boy a message to take to the first mate, who stood at the bow. The lad was only ten when he started; his white beard swabbed the deck by the time he'd reached the mast. I didn't wait to see if he lived long enough to make it the rest of the way."

His friends looked at each other. One said:

"That's nothing. You didn't need to leave home to find sights like that. Why, in the forest just over that ridge, I've seen a tree so tall that it poked a hole in the sky. Once a bird tried to fly over the top, but by the time it reached just the third branch from the bottom, it was too old to go any further. So it stopped and laid an egg, and told its chick to continue the journey. Seven generations of birds have been flying toward the top, and they're not halfway yet."

"That's ridiculous," the traveler scoffed. "I've never heard such a lie in my life."

"If that's the case," asked his friend, "where did you get the tree to make the mast for your ship?"

The Piece of String
GUY DE MAUPASSANT

This story reminds us that a lie—even a little one—can kill.

Along all the roads around Goderville, peasants and their wives were coming in toward the town for it was market day.

There was a crowd in Goderville marketplace, a confusion

of men and beasts. Horns of oxen, long-napped tall hats of the richer peasants, and the women's headdresses rose above the surface of the throng. Voices, bawling, sharp, and squeaky, were mingled in barbarous never-ending clamor, dominated at times by the mighty guffaw of some broad-chested countryman having his joke, or by the long-drawn lowing of a cow tied up to the wall of a house.

It all smelled of stables, milk and manure, of hay and sweat; gave off, in fact, that terribly sour savor, human, yet bestial, characteristic of workers in the fields.

Master Hauchecorne, of Breauté, coming in to Goderville, was making his way toward the marketplace when he perceived on the ground a short piece of string. Master Hauchecorne, thrifty like every true Norman, thought that anything was worth picking up that could be put to any use; so, stooping painfully, for he suffered from rheumatism, he picked up the bit of thin cord, and was carefully rolling it up when he observed Master Malandain, the saddler, standing in his doorway, looking at him. They had once had a difference about a halter, and owed each other a grudge, for both were by nature inclined to bear malice. Master Hauchecorne was seized with a sort of shame at being thus seen by his enemy, grubbing in the mud for a bit of string. He abruptly hid his spoil under his blouse, then put it in his trouser pocket, and pretended to be still looking on the ground for something he could not find. Finally he went off toward the market, with his head poked forward, bent nearly double by his rheumatism.

He was swallowed up at once in the slow-moving, noisy

crowd, disputing over its interminable bargainings. Peasants were punching the cows, moving hither and thither, in perpetual fear of being taken in, and not daring to make up their minds; scrutinizing the seller's eye, to try and discover the deceit in the man and the blemish in his beast.

The women, placing their great baskets at their feet, had taken out their fowls, which lay on the ground with legs tied together, eyes wild with fright, and crests all scarlet.

They listened to the offers made, and held out for their prices with wooden, impassive faces; then, suddenly deciding to take the bid, would scream after the customer as he slowly walked away:

"Done with you, Master Anthime. You shall have it."

Then, little by little, the marketplace emptied, and, the Angelus ringing midday, those who lived too far away straggled into the inns.

At Jourdain's the big dining room was crowded with guests, just as the huge courtyard was crowded with vehicles of every breed, carts, cabriolets, wagonettes, tilburys, covered carts innumerable, yellow with mud, out of trim and patched, some raising their two shafts, like arms, to the sky, some with nose on the ground and tail in the air.

Right up against the diners the immense fireplace, flaming brightly, threw a mighty heat onto the backs of the right-hand row seated at table. Three jacks were turning, garnished with chickens, pigeons, and legs of mutton, and a delectable odor of roast meat and of gravy streaming over the well-browned crackling rose from the hearth, bringing joy to the heart and water to the mouth.

All the aristocracy of the plow dined at M. Jourdain's, inn-keeper and horse-dealer, a shrewd fellow, and a "warm man."

The dishes were passed, and emptied, together with mugs of golden cider. Everyone told the story of his bargains, and asked his neighbor about the crops. The weather was good for green stuff, but a little damp for corn.

Suddenly, from the courtyard in front of the house, came the roll of a drum.

All but a few, too lazy to move, jumped up at once, and flew to the doors and windows, their mouths still full and their napkins in their hands.

Finishing off the roll of his drum, the town crier shouted in staccato tones, with a scansion of phrase peculiarly out of rhythm:

"This is to inform the inhabitants of Goderville, and all others—present at the market, that there was lost this morning on the Beuzeville road between nine and ten o'clock, a black leather pocketbook, containing five hundred francs and some business papers. It should be returned—to the Town Hall immediately, or to Master Fortuné Houlbrèque at Manneville. A reward of twenty francs is offered."

The man went by, and presently the dull rumble of the drum was heard again, and then the crier's voice, fainter in the distance.

Everyone began discussing the event, calculating the chances of Master Houlbrèque's recovering or not recovering his pocketbook.

And so the meal came to an end.

They were finishing their coffee when the brigadier of gendarmes appeared at the door, and asked:

"Is Master Hauchecorne, of Breauté, here?"

Master Hauchecorne, seated at the far end of the table, answered:

"Here!"

"Master Hauchecorne," proceeded the officer, "will you be so good as to come with me to the Town Hall? The mayor would like to speak to you."

Surprised and uneasy, the peasant gulped down his cognac, rose, and stooping even more than in the morning (for the first steps after resting were always particularly painful), got himself started, repeating:

"All right! I'm coming!" and following the sergeant.

The mayor was awaiting him, seated in an armchair. He was the notary of the district, a stout, serious man, full of pompous phrases.

"Master Hauchecorne," said he, "you were seen this morning to pick up, on the Beuzeville road, the pocketbook lost by Master Houlbrèque, of Manneville."

The peasant, in stupefaction, gazed at the mayor, intimidated at once by this suspicion which lay heavy upon him without his comprehending it.

"Me? Me—me pick up that pocketbook?"

"Yes, you."

"On my word of honor, I didn't! Why, I didn't even know about it!"

"You were seen."

"Seen? I? Who saw me?"

"M. Malandain, the saddler."

Then the old man remembered, and understood. Reddening with anger, he said:

"Ah! He saw me, that animal! Well, what he saw me pick up was this string, look here, M. le Maire!"

And rummaging in his pocket, he pulled out the little piece of string.

But the mayor shook his head incredulously.

"You won't make me believe, Master Hauchecorne, that M. Malandain, a trustworthy man, took that piece of string for a pocketbook."

The enraged peasant raised his hand, spat solemnly to show his good faith, and repeated:

"It's God's truth, all the same, the sacred truth, M. le Maire. There, on my soul and honor, I say it again."

The mayor proceeded.

"After having picked up the article in question, you even went on searching in the mud, to make sure a coin or two mightn't have fallen out."

The poor old fellow choked with indignation and fear.

"To say such things! . . . How can anyone . . . telling lies like that, to undo an honest man! How can anyone?"

Protest as he would, he was not believed.

They confronted him with M. Malandain, who repeated and substantiated his story. The two abused each other for a whole hour. By his own request, Master Hauchecorne was searched. Nothing was found on him.

At last the mayor, thoroughly puzzled, dismissed him, warning him that he was going to give notice to the public prosecutor and take his instructions.

The news had spread. As he went out of the Town Hall the old man was surrounded, and all sorts of serious or mocking questions were put to him, but no one showed the slightest indignation. He began to tell the story of the piece of string. They did not believe him. Everybody laughed.

He went on, stopped by everyone, stopping everyone he knew, to tell his story over and over again, protesting, showing his pockets turned inside out, to prove that he had nothing on him. The only answer he got was:

"Get along, you sly old dog!"

He began to feel angry, worrying himself into a fever of irritation, miserable at not being believed, at a loss what to do, and continually repeating his story. Night came on. It was time to go home. He set out with three neighbors, to whom he showed the spot where he had picked up the piece of string; and the whole way home he kept talking of his misadventure.

In the evening he made a round of the village of Breauté, to tell everybody all about it. He came across unbelievers only.

He was ill all night.

The next day, about one o'clock, Marius Paumelle, a laborer at Master Breton's, a farmer at Ymauville, restored the pocketbook and its contents to Master Houlbrèque, of Manneville.

The man declared that he found the object on the road; but not being able to read, he had taken it home and given it to his master.

The news spread through the neighborhood. Master Hauchecorne was informed of it, and started off at once on a round, to tell his story all over again, with its proper ending. It was a triumph.

"What knocked me over," he said, "was not so much the thing itself, you know, but that charge of lying. There's nothing hurts a man so much as being thought a liar."

The whole day long he talked of his adventure, telling it to people he met on the roads, to people drinking at the inns, and even at the church door on the following Sunday. He stopped perfect strangers to tell [them] about it. He was easy in his mind now, and yet—there was something that bothered him, though he could not exactly arrive at what it was. People had an amused look while they were listening to him. They did not seem convinced. He felt as if a lot of tattle was going on behind his back.

On the Tuesday of the following week he went off to Goderville market, urged thereto solely by the desire to tell his story. Malandain, standing at his door, began to laugh as he went past. Why?

He began his story to a farmer of Criquetot, who did not let him finish, but, giving him a dig in the pit of the stomach, shouted in his face: "Get along, you old rogue!" and turned his back.

Master Hauchecorne stopped short, confused, and more and more uneasy. Why was he being called an "old rogue?"

When he was seated at the table at Jourdain's inn he began again to explain the whole affair.

A horse-dealer from Montvillier called out:

"Come, come, that's an old trick; I know all about your piece of string!"

Hauchecorne stammered:

"But it's been found, that pocketbook!"

But the other went on:

"Oh! shut up, old boy, there's one who finds, and another who brings back. All on the strict QT."

The peasant was thunderstruck. He understood at last. It was insinuated that he had caused the pocketbook to be taken by someone else, an accomplice.

He tried to protest, but the whole table began laughing.

He could not finish his dinner, and went away, with every one jeering at him.

He returned home, ashamed and indignant, choking with anger and bewilderment, and all the more overwhelmed because, in his artful Norman brain, he knew himself capable of having done what they accused him of, and of even boasting about it afterward, as though it were a feat. He realized confusedly that it would be impossible to prove his innocence, his tricky nature being known to all. And he felt wounded to the heart by the injustice of this suspicion.

Then he began again to tell his story, making the tale a little longer every day, adding new reasons every time, more energetic protestations, most solemn oaths which he thought out and prepared in his solitary moments, for his mind was solely occupied by the story of the piece of string. They believed him less and less as his defense became more and more elaborate, his arguments more subtle.

"H'm! That's only to cover up his tracks," the hearers would say behind his back.

He was conscious of all this, but went on eating his heart out, exhausting himself in fruitless efforts.

Before the very eyes of people, he wasted away.

Jokers now would make him tell them the "piece of string" to amuse them, as one makes old soldiers tell about their battles. His spirit, undetermined, grew feebler and feebler.

Toward the end of December he took to his bed.

He died at the beginning of January, and in his last delirium still protested his innocence, repeating:

"A little piece of string . . . a little piece of string . . . look, here it is, M. le Maire!"

The Question

Look for honesty in yourself before you seek it in your neighbors.

> Were the whole world good as you—
> not an atom better—
> Were it just as pure and true,

Just as pure and true as you;
Just as strong in faith and works;
Just as free from crafty quirks;
All extortion, all deceit;
Schemes its neighbors to defeat;
Schemes its neighbors to defraud;
Schemes some culprit to applaud—
Would this world be better?

If the whole world followed you—
followed to the letter—
Would it be a nobler world,
All deceit and falsehood hurled
From it altogether;
Malice, selfishness, and lust,
Banished from beneath the crust,
Covering human hearts from view—
Tell me, if it followed you,
Would the world be better?

The Story of Regulus

RETOLD BY JAMES BALDWIN

This ancient story is about the Roman general and states-
man Marcus Atilius Regulus. It takes place in the third

century B.C. during the First Punic War between Rome and Carthage. The legend of how Regulus kept his word made him famous in Roman history.

On the other side of the sea from Rome there was once a great city named Carthage. The Roman people were never very friendly to the people of Carthage, and at last a war began between them. For a long time it was hard to tell which would prove the stronger. First the Romans would gain a battle, and then the men of Carthage would gain a battle; and so the war went on for many years.

Among the Romans there was a brave general named Regulus—a man of whom it was said that he never broke his word. It so happened after a while that Regulus was taken prisoner and carried to Carthage. Ill and very lonely, he dreamed of his wife and little children so far away beyond the sea; and he had but little hope of ever seeing them again. He loved his home dearly, but he believed that his first duty was to his country; and so he had left all to fight in this cruel war.

He had lost a battle, it is true, and had been taken prisoner. Yet he knew that the Romans were gaining ground, and the people of Carthage were afraid of being beaten in the end. They had sent into other countries to hire soldiers to help them. But even with these they would not be able to fight much longer against Rome.

One day some of the rulers of Carthage came to the prison to talk with Regulus.

"We should like to make peace with the Roman people," they said, "and we are sure that, if your rulers at home knew how the war is going, they would be glad to make peace with us. We will set you free and let you go home, if you will agree to do as we say."

"What is that?" asked Regulus.

"In the first place," they said, "you must tell the Romans about the battles which you have lost, and you must make it plain to them that they have not gained anything by the war. In the second place, you must promise us that, if they will not make peace, you will come back to your prison."

"Very well," said Regulus. "I promise you that if they will not make peace, I will come back to prison."

And so they let him go, for they knew that a great Roman would keep his word.

When he came to Rome, all the people greeted him gladly. His wife and children were very happy, for they thought that now they would not be parted again. The white-haired Fathers who made the laws for the city came to see him. They asked him about the war.

"I was sent from Carthage to ask you to make peace," he said. "But it will not be wise to make peace. True, we have been beaten in a few battles, but our army is gaining ground every day. The people of Carthage are afraid, and well they may be. Keep on with the war a little while longer, and Carthage shall be yours. As for me, I have come to bid my wife and children and Rome farewell. Tomorrow I will start back to Carthage and to prison, for I have promised."

Then the Fathers tried to persuade him to stay.

"Let us send another man in your place," they said.

"Shall a Roman not keep his word?" answered Regulus. "I am ill, and at the best have not long to live. I will go back as I promised."

His wife and little children wept, and his sons begged him not to leave them again.

"I have given my word," said Regulus. "The rest will be taken care of."

Then he bade them goodbye, and went bravely back to the prison and the cruel death which he expected.

This was the kind of courage that made Rome the greatest city in the world.

Truth and Falsehood

As this folktale from Greece points out, the virtuous soul not only loves truth for its own sake, it loathes the actions of falsehood. Deceit is far more painful for that soul than bearing the hardships that sometimes accompany honesty.

Once upon a time Truth and Falsehood met each other on the road.

"Good afternoon," said Truth.

"Good afternoon," returned Falsehood. "And how are you doing these days?"

"Not very well at all, I'm afraid," sighed Truth. "The times are tough for a fellow like me, you know."

"Yes, I can see that," said Falsehood, glancing up and down at Truth's ragged clothes. "You look like you haven't had a bite to eat in quite some time."

"To be honest, I haven't," admitted Truth. "No one seems to want to employ me nowadays. Wherever I go, most people ignore me or mock me. It's getting discouraging, I can tell you. I'm beginning to ask myself why I put up with it."

"And why the devil do you? Come with me, and I'll show you how to get along. There's no reason in the world why you can't stuff yourself with as much as you want to eat, like me, and dress in the finest clothes, like me. But you must promise not to say a word against me while we're together."

So Truth promised and agreed to go along with Falsehood for a while, not because he liked his company so much, but because he was so hungry he thought he'd faint soon if he didn't get something into his stomach. They walked down the road until they came to a city, and Falsehood at once led the way to the very best table at the very best restaurant.

"Waiter, bring us your choicest meats, your sweetest sweets, your finest wine!" he called, and they ate and drank all afternoon. At last, when they could hold no more, Falsehood began banging his fist on the table and calling for the manager, who came running at once.

"What the devil kind of place is this?" Falsehood snapped. "I gave that waiter a gold piece nearly an hour ago, and he still hasn't brought our change."

The manager summoned the waiter, who said he'd never even seen a penny out of the gentleman.

"What?" Falsehood shouted, so that everyone in the place turned and looked. "I can't believe this place! Innocent, law-abiding citizens come in to eat, and you rob them of their hard-earned money! You're a pack of thieves and liars! You may have fooled me once, but you'll never see me again! Here!" He threw a gold piece at the manager. "Now this time bring me my change!"

But the manager, fearing his restaurant's reputation would suffer, refused to take the gold piece, and instead brought Falsehood change for the first gold piece he claimed to have spent. Then he took the waiter aside and called him a scoundrel, and said he had a mind to fire him. And as much as the waiter protested that he'd never collected a cent from the man, the manager refused to believe him.

"Oh, Truth, where have you hidden yourself?" the waiter sighed. "Have you now deserted even us hard-working souls?"

"No, I'm here," Truth groaned to himself, "but my judgment gave way to my hunger, and now I can't speak up without breaking my promise to Falsehood."

As soon as they were on the street, Falsehood gave a hearty laugh and slapped Truth on the back. "You see how the world works?" he cried. "I managed it all quite well, don't you think?"

But Truth slipped from his side.

"I'd rather starve than live as you do," he said.

And so Truth and Falsehood went their separate ways, and never traveled together again.

Truth, Falsehood, Fire, and Water

This tale about the eternal struggle between truth and false-
hood is told in Ethiopia and other eastern African nations.

Long ago Truth, Falsehood, Fire, and Water were journeying
together and came upon a herd of cattle. They talked it over and
decided it would be fairest to divide the herd into four parts, so
each could take home an equal share.

But Falsehood was greedy and schemed to get more for himself.

"Listen to my warning," he whispered, pulling Water to one
side. "Fire plans to burn all the grass and trees along your banks
and drive your cattle away across the plains so he can have them
for himself. If I were you, I'd extinguish him now, and then we can
have his share of the cattle for ourselves."

Water was foolish enough to listen to Falsehood, and he
dashed himself upon Fire and put him out.

Next Falsehood crept toward Truth.

"Look what Water has done," he whispered. "He has murdered
Fire and taken his cattle. We should not consort with the likes of
him. We should take all the cattle and go to the mountains."

Truth believed Falsehood and agreed to his plan. Together
they drove the cattle into the mountains.

"Wait for me!" Water called, and he hurried after them, but
of course he could not run uphill. So he was left all alone in the
valley below.

When they reached the top of the highest mountain, Falsehood turned to Truth and laughed.

"I've tricked you, stupid fool," he shrieked. "Now you must give me all the cattle and be my servant, or I'll destroy you."

"Yes, you have tricked me," Truth admitted, "but I will never be your servant."

And so they fought, and when they clashed the thunder rolled back and forth across the mountain tops. Again and again they threw themselves together, but neither could destroy the other.

Finally they decided to call upon the Wind to declare a winner of the contest. So Wind came rushing up the mountain slopes, and he listened to what they had to say.

"It is not for me to declare a winner in this fight," he told them. "Truth and Falsehood are destined to struggle. Sometimes Truth will win, but other times Falsehood will prevail, and then Truth must rise up and fight again. Until the end of the world. Truth must battle Falsehood, and must never rest or let down his guard, or he will be finished once and for all."

And so Truth and Falsehood are fighting to this day.

LOYALTY

Loyalty

The great Jewish teacher Rabbi Hillel once asked: "If I am not for myself, who is for me? But if I am only for myself, what am I?"

You should ask yourself those same questions when thinking about loyalty. It is certainly important to care about yourself, to think of your own needs, to "look out for number one." But if that is *all* you care about, or if that is what you care about the *most,* what kind of person does that make you?

Loyalty means caring in a serious way about your relationships with others and being willing to show it through your actions. You can have loyalty to many people or groups—to family, to friends, to your school, to your church, to your country. In all these cases, loyalty means looking past your own needs. It means putting yourself in second place, if necessary. It requires that you do the right thing at the right time for those you care about.

We often say that we "owe our loyalty" to someone or something. That's because relationships are a two-way street. We want to show we care about certain people in part because they have shown they care about us. Eleanor Roosevelt put it this way: "Up to a certain point it is good for us to know that there are people in the world who will give us love and unquestioned loyalty to the limit of their ability. I doubt, however, if it is good for us to feel assured of this without the accompanying obligation of having to justify this devotion by our behavior."

Children can show loyalty to their parents, for example, by behaving with respect and obedience. Parents, in return, do everything they can to take care of their children and act in their best interests.

Husbands and wives show loyalty to each other in part through their faithfulness to one another. Fidelity in marriage is an expression of love. It is a kind of loyalty that helps make a marriage a sacred relationship.

Friends show loyalty by being honest and dependable with each other. Loyalty to a friend, by the way, does not mean doing whatever your friend asks you to do. It means, rather, doing what will help your friend become a better person.

Loyalty to team means showing up for practice on time and giving your best efforts. And, in return, you expect your teammates to do the same.

Loyalty to country—patriotism—involves obeying its laws, upholding its principles, and even defending those principles if necessary. Citizens owe such loyalty in return for the protection of their rights and privileges as well as for the many opportunities that their country has offered them.

When you say the Pledge of Allegiance to the flag, you are literally giving an oath of loyalty, not to a piece of cloth but to a symbol. For your pledge to mean anything, you need to know a few things about "the Republic for which it stands." For example, you need to know something about its Constitution, its government, its history, and its traditions. Otherwise, you are simply swearing blind allegiance.

In all of these cases, loyalty means that you are ready to put another before yourself. In an age when people are told to "do what feels good," or "do your own thing," loyalty reminds us that often we should be doing something for someone else. As Woodrow Wilson said, "Loyalty means nothing unless it has at its heart the absolute principle of self-sacrifice." That self-sacrifice is, in the end, what gives serious meaning to our relationships.

A Brother in Need

Loyalty begins at home, as this Vietnamese tale reminds us.

There were once two brothers, Gan and Duc, whose father died suddenly, without leaving a will. Gan, the older brother, took all the land and property for himself except for one small shack and one miserable patch of acreage, which he allowed Duc to have. Duc's field was so tiny it could produce barely enough for him to eat, and year after year he grew poorer and thinner despite his hard work. Gan's green field, meanwhile, flourished every year until he was the wealthiest man in the province.

The richer Gan grew, the more friends he discovered. They came to see him night and day, and he never hesitated to serve lavish meals, pour his best wines, and give away expensive tokens of affection. "I'll do anything for a friend in need," Gan was fond of saying.

Now, Gan had a kind-hearted wife named Hanh who could not understand why her husband treated his own brother so cruelly.

"You say there's nothing you wouldn't do for your friends," she pointed out, "and yet look at the way you let your brother live."

"I have nothing to do with the way he lives," Gan snapped. "He can fend for himself, just as I have. Besides, my friends rank among the finest people in the province. It's only fitting that I treat them according to what they deserved."

"Nevertheless, he is your brother. And I'm sure if you treated him as your friend, you'd find more devotion in him than in these friends you treat as brothers."

But this conversation took place many times, and Gan never listened.

One evening Gan came home to find his wife in tears.

"What's happened?" he asked.

"Something horrible," she sobbed. "This afternoon a beggar came to the door and asked for something to eat. He looked so weak and pale, I couldn't say no. So I told him to step inside while I got something from the kitchen. But no sooner did the poor man cross our threshold than he fainted from hunger. He struck his head on the table and fell dead on the floor. I was so frightened, I wrapped his body in a blanket and dragged it into the garden."

"But there's nothing to worry about," Gan assured her. "You did nothing wrong. We'll explain the situation to the mandarin. You were just trying to help."

"You're wrong," Hanh cried. "The mandarin has never liked you. He's jealous of your riches and popularity. He'll use this chance to ruin us, if he can."

At this Gan turned pale himself. He remembered how stern and cold the mandarin had always been, and how he never accepted Gan's invitations to come dine.

"What will we do then?" he asked, ringing his hands.

"I've thought of a plan," Hanh whispered. "Tonight you must bury the beggar deep in the forest, where no one will find him. Choose your most devoted friend to help you and swear him to secrecy."

So Gan hurried to the home of the man who had dined most at his table. His friend greeted him with a warm embrace and an eager smile. But when Gan explained in low tones how he needed help, his friend shook his head and backed away. He was sorry, he'd love more than anything to help, but his back was giving him problems, and he couldn't possibly carry the load of a dead man through the forest.

Gan hurried to another friend's house, where once again he was warmly received.

"It's been too long!" the friend gushed. "Tell me now, how can I help you?"

"I knew I could count on you." Gan sighed. "You were always the best of friends. Something horrible has happened." But as he told his story, his friend's expression changed.

"I wish I could help, Gan, you know I do," he lamented. "But the fact is, my poor old grandmother is ill tonight and may even be on her deathbed. I can't possibly leave her. I knew you'd understand."

And so it went, from door to door, from friend to friend. Some had sick relatives, some were ill themselves, others had pressing engagements. None were able to help, and Gan trudged home alone, trembling with fear and disappointment.

His wife listened to what happened and said:

"There's no time to lose. You don't have a choice. You must go ask your brother for help."

Gan knew she was right—there was no one else now. He hurried into the night again and found his brother's humble house.

Duc could not conceal his surprise when he opened his door. Then he saw the anguish on his brother's face.

"What's wrong?" he asked at once. "You look half-dead. Are you sick? Is Hanh all right?"

In faltering words, Gan told why he had come. Before he had finished, Duc was putting on his jacket. The two brothers rushed back to Gan's house, found the shrouded body in the garden, and hauled it into the woods. The sun was rising by the time they'd buried the secret burden and staggered home again.

They were stunned to find one of the mandarin's men waiting for them.

"You are to come with me," he ordered Gan, "along with your wife and brother."

They were taken to the mandarin's house, and there they found gathered all the friends whose help Gan had begged. One by one the informers stepped forward and told how they had refused to take part in the brothers' foul crime.

"Not only are you murderers," the mandarin said, "you tried to talk your friends into concealing your misdeed. Thankfully, your friends are better men than you. They are honest, and they are loyal to me. They followed you into the forest and then came to report your crime. So there's no use in denying it. We'll go retrieve the body, and then you'll get what is due."

The entire crowd trooped into the forest, and the hastily dug grave was uncovered. There was a gasp when the blanket was unwrapped and the corpse of an old ram, not a beggar, fell out.

"What is the meaning of this?" the mandarin demanded.

Gan and Duc stood as confused as the rest. Their accusers glanced at each other nervously.

Then Hanh stepped forward.

"This is my doing," she confessed. "For a long time I've watched my husband treat his brother like a stranger while he spared nothing on his friends. I could see how those friends hung on to him only because of the food and wine they could have at his expense. I wanted to prove to him that there can be no loyalty greater than a brother's. So yesterday, when this old ram of ours died, I invented a plan to open my husband's eyes. And here we are."

Gan's accusers looked at their feet, while the mandarin stood silent for a moment.

"You are a wise woman," he said at last. "This lesson is worth a night's inconvenience."

From then on, Gan and Duc lived as brothers should.

America the Beautiful
KATHARINE LEE BATES

Massachusetts educator and author Katharine Lee Bates wrote "America the Beautiful" in 1893 after being inspired by the view from Pikes Peak in Colorado. She revised the lyrics to their final form in 1911. They are set to the music of Samuel A. Ward's "Materna."

O beautiful for spacious skies,
For amber waves of grain,
For purple mountain majesties
Above the fruited plain!
America! America!
God shed His grace on thee
And crown thy good with brotherhood
From sea to shining sea!

O beautiful for Pilgrim feet,
Whose stern, impassioned stress
A thoroughfare for freedom beat
Across the wilderness!
America! America!
God mend thine every flaw,
Confirm thy soul in self-control,
Thy liberty in law!

O beautiful for heroes proved
In liberating strife,
Who more than self their country loved,
And mercy more than life!
America! America!
May God thy gold refine,
Till all success be nobleness
And every gain divine!

O beautiful for patriot dream
That sees beyond the years
Thine alabaster cities gleam
Undimmed by human tears!
America! America!
God shed His grace on thee,
And crown thy good with brotherhood
From sea to shining sea!

Barbara Frietchie

JOHN GREENLEAF WHITTIER

Sometimes our sense of loyalty demands that we show the flag even in the enemy's midst. John Greenleaf Whittier (1807-1892) wrote this poem in 1863, during the Civil War, and claimed its story is true.

Up from the meadows rich with corn,
Clear in the cool September morn,

The clustered spires of Frederick stand
Green-walled by the hills of Maryland.

Round about them orchards sweep,
Apple and peach tree fruited deep,

Fair as the garden of the Lord
To the eyes of the famished rebel horde,

On that pleasant morn of the early fall
When Lee marched over the mountain wall;

Over the mountains winding down,
Horse and foot, into Frederick town.

Forty flags with their silver stars,
Forty flags with their crimson bars,

Flapped in the morning wind: the sun
Of noon looked down, and saw not one.

Up rose old Barbara Frietchie then,
Bowed with her fourscore years and ten;

Bravest of all in Frederick town,
She took up the flag the men hauled down;

In her attic window the staff she set,
To show that one heart was loyal yet.

Up the street came the rebel tread,
Stonewall Jackson riding ahead.

Under his slouched hat left and right
He glanced; the old flag met his sight.

"Halt"—the dust-brown ranks stood fast.
"Fire"—out blazed the rifle blast.

It shivered the window, pane and sash;
It rent the banner with seam and gash.

Quick, as it fell, from the broken staff
Dame Barbara snatched the silken scarf.

She leaned far out on the windowsill,
And shook it forth with a royal will.

"Shoot, if you must, this old gray head,
But spare your country's flag," she said.

A shade of sadness, a blush of shame,
Over the face of the leader came;

The nobler nature within him stirred
To life at that woman's deed and word;

"Who touches a hair on yon gray head
Dies like a dog! March on!" he said.

All day long through Frederick street
Sounded the tread of marching feet:

All day long that free flag tost
Over the heads of the rebel host.

Even its torn folds rose and fell
On the loyal winds that loved it well;

And through the hill gaps sunset light
Shone over it with a warm good night.

Barbara Frietchie's work is o'er,
And the Rebel rides on his raids no more.

Honor to her! and let a tear
Fall, for her sake, on Stonewall's bier.

Over Barbara Frietchie's grave
Flag of Freedom and Union, wave!

Peace and order and beauty draw
Round thy symbol of light and law;

And ever the stars above look down
On thy stars below in Frederick town!

Castor and Pollux

The Greek writer Menander said that to live is not to live
for one's self alone. The story of Castor and Pollux helps us
understand this meaning of the word brotherhood.

On winter nights the constellation Gemini lies high overhead,
and its two principal stars, Castor and Pollux, are among the bright-
est in the heavens. We know them as the Twins, but old myths from
the days of Greek heroes say they were really half brothers. Leda
was the mother of both, while Castor's father was Tyndareus, the
king of Sparta, and Pollux's father was Zeus, king of the gods. So the
span of Castor's life was fixed, but Pollux was immortal.

By all accounts, the brothers were never apart, so great
was their devotion to each other, and they shared many adventures. They sailed with Jason and the Argonauts on the quest for
the Golden Fleece, and they rescued their sister Helen when
she was kidnapped by Theseus, the same beautiful Helen whose
face later "launched a thousand ships" and brought about the
Trojan War. They also took part in the famous Calydonian hunt,
in which many of Greece's bravest heroes gathered to rid the
land of a monstrous boar.

The most famous legend about Castor and Pollux is about how
they ended their earthly lives. The Greek poet Pindar tells us that
Castor was wounded in battle. His brother rushed to his side, only to
find him almost dead, gasping out his life with short-drawn breath.

Pollux did everything he could to save him, but there was no hope.

"Oh father Zeus," Pollux cried, "take my life instead of my brother's! Or if not that, let me die also! Without him, I will know nothing but grief for the rest of my days."

As he spoke, Zeus approached and answered. "You are my son, Pollux, and therefore enjoy eternal life. Your brother was born of mortal seed, and destined like all humans to taste death. But I will give you a choice. You may come to Olympus, as is your right, and dwell with Athena and Ares and the rest of the gods. Or, if you wish to share your immortality with your brother, then half the time you must spend beneath the earth, and the other half in the golden home of heaven."

Pollux did not for an instant waver, but gave up his life in Olympus, and chose to share light and darkness forever with his brother. So Zeus unclosed Castor's eyes and restored his breath. And even now we see them as the constellation Gemini. They spend half their time fixed in the starry heavens, and the other half sunk beneath the horizon.

Fading Favor

This Chinese tale reminds us that our fidelities should not change because another's physical appearance changes. In many marriage vows, people say "till death do us part," not "till age do us part."

In olden days there was a king who liked to keep his court filled with ladies from all over the land. His favorite was a beautiful young maiden named Hua.

"Ah, Hua," he used to say, "you are the most wondrous creature under the blue heavens. Someday you shall be my queen."

This king kept a stern law that anyone who rode his horse without his permission would be punished by death. One day, when Hua suddenly learned her mother was ill, she jumped on the horse and rode off to the old woman's bedside.

"What devotion!" The king sighed. "To think she risked her own life to tend to her poor mother!"

Another time, Hua and the king were strolling in the royal garden. Hua picked a plum and took a bite; its flavor was so splendid, she handed it to the king to taste.

"What loyalty," he thought. "She discovers this perfect fruit and would rather give it to me to enjoy than finish it herself!"

But eventually Hua's beauty began to fade, and with it the king's affections.

"Didn't she once take my horse, even though she knew it was a crime?" he remembered. "And another time she handed me the remains of a plum after chewing on it herself!"

He decided to choose a younger woman as his queen.

How Queen Esther Saved Her People

RETOLD BY WALTER RUSSELL BOWIE

The events of the book of Esther in the Bible are reported to have occurred during the reign of the Persian king Ahasuerus, whom biblical scholars usually identify with Xerxes (c. 519-465 B.C.). Esther and her kinsman Mordecai were members of the Jewish population remaining in the East after many other Jews had returned to Jerusalem from the Babylonian exile. The story is one of a young queen who must face danger alone to save her people.

The story of the book of Esther begins with one of the kings of Persia, who is called Ahasuerus. According to the story, Ahasuerus decided one day to have a great feast in the garden of his palace. He invited all the chief men of the kingdom to come. The garden court was a beautiful place within the palace walls. It had marble pillars and a pavement of red, blue, white, and black marble. There were hangings of white and green and blue, fastened on silver rings. The goblets in which the wine was served were gold.

The feasting went on for seven days. By that time everyone, including the king, had eaten and drunk a great deal too much. The queen, whose name was Vashti, was very beautiful. Suddenly the king had a notion that he would show her off to his guests. She was in her rooms with her maids. The king sent seven of his servants to tell the queen to come to the feast.

Vashti was ashamed and indignant that the king had sent her such a message. She had no intention of appearing before a large company of half-drunken men. She told the servants to tell the king that she would not come.

When the king heard that, he was furious. He had boasted of the queen's beauty. Now he would seem foolish in the sight of his guests. He asked some of them what they thought he ought to do. These men did not have much respect for women. They began to think that if their wives heard that the queen had disobeyed the king, they would disobey their husbands. The men told the king that he ought to get rid of Vashti and find a new queen.

That was exactly what Ahasuerus decided to do. He sent Vashti away. Then came the question of choosing a new queen. The king's servants looked everywhere in the kingdom, and brought to the palace the most beautiful maidens they could find. Among them was a maiden from a Jewish family, whose name was Esther. She was young and innocent and lovely, and could never have dreamed that she might become the queen of Persia. When the king saw Esther, he preferred her to everyone else, and he made her his wife. But he did not know that she had come from among the Jews.

Now Esther had a cousin named Mordecai. Mordecai, who was older than Esther, had brought her up like a daughter because her own father was dead. Esther trusted him in everything, and whatever he advised her to do, she did. Mordecai told her not to tell the king that she was a Jew.

Mordecai came often to the palace, to speak with Esther. Often he would sit in the gate where people went in and out and where they stood together talking. One day he saw two men who were plainly very angry. They talked excitedly, and Mordecai overheard what they were saying. They were plotting together to kill the king.

Mordecai sent word of that to Esther, and Esther warned the king. The king had the two men arrested and put to death. By his warning, Mordecai had saved the king's life. The king should have been very grateful, but he was more interested in himself than in anyone else. Although he had been told that it was Mordecai who had brought the warning, he soon forgot it.

Meanwhile there was another man who was becoming the king's favorite. His name was Haman. The king's servants had to bow to Haman whenever he passed by. But Mordecai would not bow to Haman or give any sign that he noticed him at all. Every day Mordecai was warned that he would find himself in trouble if he did not do as the king's servants did, but Mordecai paid no attention. After a while someone asked Haman if he had noticed that Mordecai, the Jew, never bowed to him when he went by. The very idea made Haman angry, for he was proud and jealous. To hear that anybody had dared not show respect to him was more than he would stand. He began to consider what would be the worst thing he would do to Mordecai. He thought about it for some time. Finally he decided that there was something worse than having Mordecai punished alone. Since Mordecai was a Jew, Haman would make all the Jewish people suffer.

So one day Haman went to the king and poured into his ears all the ugly tales he could think of about the Jews. He reminded Ahasuerus that the Jews were scattered all through the kingdom.

He said there were entirely too many of them for the kingdom's good. Had the king stopped to remember that the Jews were different from the people of Persia, and had different laws? He suggested getting rid of these Jewish people who might turn out to be enemies of Persia. And Haman said that he would put ten thousand talents of silver, a huge amount of money, into the king's treasury if the king would sign an order that all the Jews should be destroyed.

Ahasuerus not only had a quick temper but he was stupid, too. He believed everything that Haman told him. He flew into a rage against the Jews and told Haman to have them killed.

Haman heard that with wicked pleasure. He lost no time in making sure that what he had planned should happen. He sent out orders, in the king's name and with the king's seal, to the governors of all the parts of the kingdom. These orders commanded that on a certain day every Jewish person—man, woman, and child—should be put to death. Then Haman went in and sat down to drink wine with the king, and to rejoice.

Out in the city the people who had begun to hear the news were shocked and troubled. Before long the news reached Mordecai. He dressed himself in rough sackcloth and poured ashes on his head as a sign of distress. Then he went to the gate of the palace to weep and mourn.

One of the palace maids told Esther of this. Esther was greatly troubled. She sent to Mordecai to beg him to take off his sackcloth, and to let her know quickly what was wrong. Mordecai told the messenger the terrible truth—that all the Jews in the kingdom were in danger of death. Only she might save them by going to the king and begging him to change the order.

Esther seemed to be faced with more than a woman could bear. She was the queen, but she knew only too well the cruel laws of the Persian court. She knew that no one, least of all a woman, might dare to cross the king. Esther sent the messenger back to Mordecai. Did he not know that if anyone went to the king uninvited, he might be put to death? This would certainly happen unless the king was in good humor and held out his golden scepter as a sign of permission to come near. Esther had no reason to think that the king would treat her so kindly. It had been many days since he had sent for her and since she had seen him.

Mordecai sent back word that there was only one hope for the Jews in Persia; only one person could do anything, and that person was Esther. She must not think, Mordecai added, that if the king's order for the killing of Jews was carried out she would escape. It would be found out that she too was a Jew, and she would be treated like the rest. But she alone might be able to do what everyone else put together could not do. Perhaps this was her chance to show a kind of courage that few would dare to show. "Who knows," said Mordecai, "but that you have come to the kingdom for such a time as this?"

When Esther received Mordecai's message, all her heart rose bravely to answer. So much depended on her that she could not be timid anymore. She sent word back to Mordecai that he should gather the Jews together to fast and pray. She and her maids in the palace would do the same. Then she would go to the king and try to persuade him. "And if I perish," she said, "I perish."

The moment came when she must take the great and final risk. Ahasuerus, in all his pomp and power, was sitting on his royal throne. Esther dressed herself in her queenliest robes. She went to the door of the throne room. The door was opened, and she stood there, beautiful and silent, waiting, looking at the king. If he were angry, that would be the end.

But the king stretched out the golden scepter toward her. "Queen Esther!" he said. "What will you have? What is your request? It shall be given you, even if it be half of the kingdom!"

So the king was not angry! He was fond of her, and perhaps he would listen to her more than he had listened to the wicked Haman. But she would not tell her real wish now. Instead, she said, "If it seems good to the king, will he, and Haman also, come to a banquet which I have made ready today?"

The king said that he would come, and that Haman should come, too.

When they were seated at the table, the king told Esther again that he would give her anything she wanted, no matter what it might be. But she begged him not to have her tell him then what she wanted. Would he wait until tomorrow? And would he and Haman come to another banquet the next day? Yes, the king said, they would come.

Haman went out, proud and pleased. He had been invited to a banquet alone with the king and queen, and he was invited again tomorrow! But as he left the palace, there, sitting at the gate, was

Mordecai. Mordecai did not stand up or bow, or even notice him. That spoiled everything. Haman snapped his lips shut and walked by Mordecai without a word. When he reached home he called his wife and some of his friends, and broke into a storm of complaining. He told them all of the honors the king had given him, and that anybody could see how great a man he was, but that this Mordecai still despised him.

Haman's wife and friends were as bad-tempered as Haman. Why did he not go at once and ask the king's permission to hang Mordecai? "Ask the king to make a gallows fifty cubits high," they said. That seemed to Haman a good idea. Without asking the king, he had the gallows built to hang Mordecai on.

Then things began to happen in a way Haman had not expected. That night the king could not sleep. He tossed about impatiently. Finally he decided he would read awhile, and he told one of his servants to bring him a book. The book the servant happened to bring was a history of the events of the king's court during the last few years. The king commanded that the book be read aloud to him. As he listened, he heard about the two men who had plotted to kill him, and how Mordecai had overheard them and had given warning.

Suddenly the king remembered that he had never rewarded Mordecai for this. It annoyed him to think that he had forgotten about it all this time. He asked his servants, "What about this Mordecai? What has been done for him?"

They told him, "Nothing."

"Who is in the court right now?" the king asked.

It happened that at just that moment Haman had come to the palace to tell the king about the gallows he had had built for Mordecai. The servants told the king that Haman was outside.

"Let him come in," said the king.

So Haman came in. The king's mind was full of what he had been hearing. "Haman," he asked, "what ought to be done to a man whom the king wants very much to honor?"

He means me! thought Haman. He tried not to look excited.

"What ought to be done for a man whom the king wants very much to honor?" Haman repeated. "Let royal robes be brought like those which the king wears, and the king's horse, too, and the king's own crown. Let these be put in charge of one of the noblest of the princes. Let the prince put the royal robes on the man the king has chosen to honor. Then the prince shall lead this man, on horseback, through the city and proclaim to the people that he is the man whom the king delights to honor."

"Good!" said the king. "Now hurry and do exactly as you have said. Take one of my royal robes and have the king's horse brought. Find Mordecai the Jew and lead him through the city."

If the king had struck Haman with a hammer between the eyes, Haman could not have been more stunned. But there was no escape from what the king had commanded, and Haman did not dare even to look surprised. In a black and bitter fury he had to go out and give Mordecai the honors he had supposed were meant for him. He held the bridle of the king's horse, with Mordecai riding on it, dressed in a royal robe. And he had to cry to the people who crowded the streets, "This is the man whom the king delights to honor!"

But that was not all. The banquet with the king and queen was still to come.

When the three of them were sitting there together, Ahasuerus asked Esther again what she wanted him to do for her. This time she really told him. She reminded him of the order that had gone out in his name that all the Jews in the kingdom should be killed. Then she told him that she herself belonged to the Jewish people. She pleaded that he would take back that dreadful order and spare them. "If I have found favor in your sight," she said, "grant me this petition!"

When the king looked at Esther, so lovely and so distressed, he was angry to think that he had been tricked by someone, he had almost forgotten who, into giving that order. "Who has done this?" he demanded. "Where is he?"

Then Esther the queen looked straight at Haman. "It is this wicked Haman," she said.

The king was so full of rage that he got up and strode out into the garden. Haman was terrified, and he fell down on the couch where the queen was sitting. In came the king again at that moment, and he thought Haman was trying to hurt the queen. "What!" he cried. "Will he attack the queen here in my own palace?" He called his servants, and they took Haman out.

One of the king's officers came and asked the king if he knew that Haman had built a gallows near his own house, a gallows nearly a hundred feet high. No, the king had not known it, but now that he knew, he knew also what should be done with it. "Take Haman and hang him on it," he commanded. So on the very gallows which he had intended for Mordecai, Haman himself was hanged.

That is the story of the book of Esther. And from that day the Jewish people, who had suffered a great deal, were glad to remember the truthful Mordecai and the young queen who, all alone, carried through a dangerous duty.

Loyalty to a Brother
WALTER MACPEEK

Family loyalties involve certain obligations. They are duties we perform out of love, as this simple story from an old Boy Scout book reminds us.

One of two brothers fighting in the same company in France fell by a German bullet. The one who escaped asked permission of his officer to go and bring his brother in.

"He is probably dead," said the officer, "and there is no use in your risking your life to bring in his body."

But after further pleading the officer consented. Just as the soldier reached the lines with his brother on his shoulders, the wounded man died.

"There, you see," said the officer, "you risked your life for nothing."

"No," replied Tom. "I did what he expected of me, and I have my reward. When I crept up to him and took him in my arms, he said,

'Tom, I knew you would come—I just felt you would come.'"

There you have the gist of it all; somebody expects something fine and noble and unselfish of us; someone expects us to be faithful.

Nathan Hale
FROM AMERICAN HERITAGE MAGAZINE

Americans look to the Revolutionary War to find the two names that mark the extremes of loyalty to country. On one end of the spectrum we find Benedict Arnold, perhaps the most despised name in the nation's history. At the other end stands Nathan Hale.

Ever since he was executed by the British on the morning of September 22, 1776, the death of Nathan Hale has been recognized as one of the great moments of American patriotism. Some years ago the late George Dudley Seymour gathered all the contemporary descriptions of the young hero's career that he could find, and had them privately printed in a *Documentary Life of Nathan Hale.* In the selections below we can read at first hand, in the words of both his friends and his foes, a story that has inspired generations of Hale's countrymen.

Following his graduation from Yale in 1773 at the age of eighteen, Hale taught school for a time in his native Connecticut. Then, on July 1, 1775—two months after Lexington and Concord—he was commissioned a lieutenant in the Continental

Army, and closed his one-room school in New London, a building still proudly preserved by the town. We see him first in the reminiscences of a comrade-in-arms, Lieutenant Elisha Bostwick:

> I can now in imagination see his person and hear his voice—
> his person, I should say, was a little above the common stature
> in height, his shoulders of a moderate breadth, his limbs
> strait and very plump: regular features—very fair skin—blue
> eyes—flaxen or very light hair which was always kept
> short—his eyebrows a shade darker than his hair and his voice
> rather sharp or piercing—his bodily agility was remarkable.
> I have seen him follow a football and kick it over the tops of
> the trees in the Bowery at New York (an exercise which he
> was fond of)—his mental powers seemed to be above the
> common sort—his mind of a sedate and sober cast, and he
> was undoubtedly pious; for it was remarked that when any of
> the soldiers of his company were sick he always visited them
> and usually prayed for and with them in their sickness.

Early in the fall of 1776, after being disastrously defeated on Long Island, Washington needed to know the dispositions and the intentions of the British forces. Hale and the other officers of the picked regiment known as Knowlton's Rangers were asked to volunteer for an intelligence mission behind enemy lines. On the first call, none responded; on the second, Nathan Hale alone stepped forward. A little later he told his friend Captain (afterward General) William Hull what he had done:

[Hale] asked my candid opinion [says Hull's memoir].
I replied, that it was an action which involved serious consequences, and the propriety of it was doubtful . . .
Stratagems are resorted to in war; they are feints and
evasions, performed under no disguise . . . and, considered in a military view, lawful and advantageous . . . But
who respects the character of a spy, assuming the garb of
friendship but to betray? . . . I ended by saying, that should
he undertake the enterprise, his short, bright career would
close with an ignominious death.

He replied, "I am fully sensible of the consequences of
discovery and capture in such a situation . . . Yet . . . I wish
to be useful, and every kind of service, necessary to the
public good, becomes honorable by being necessary. If the
exigencies of my country demand a peculiar service, its
claims to perform that service are imperious."

Sergeant Stephen Hempstead of New London accompanied
him as he set out on his mission from Norwalk, Connecticut:

Captain Hale had a general order to all armed vessels to take him
to anyplace he should designate: he was set across the Sound . . .
at Huntington (Long Island) . . . Captain Hale had changed his
uniform for a plain suit of citizen's brown clothes, with a round
broad-brimmed hat, assuming the character of a Dutch schoolmaster, leaving all his other clothes, commission, public and

private papers, with me, and also his silver shoe buckles, saying they would not comport with his character of schoolmaster, and retaining nothing but his college diploma, as an introduction to his assumed calling. Thus equipped, we parted.

Hale's servant, Asher Wright, who had remained behind, told what happened next:

> He passed all their guards on Long Island, went over to New York in a ferryboat and got by all the guards but the last. They stopped him, searched and found drawings of the works, with descriptions in Latin, under the inner sole of the pumps which he wore. Some say his cousin, Samuel Hale, a Tory, betrayed him. I don't know; guess he did.

"Betrayed" is probably too strong; "identified" is closer to the truth. A surviving letter from Samuel, a Harvard man (1766), seems to deny any misdeed, or at least any guilt, as the story was spread in a Newburyport newspaper—but he thereafter fled to England and never returned to America, even after the war, for his wife and son.

The next day a kindhearted British officer, Captain John Montresor, approached the American lines under a flag of truce to report the inevitable denouement. Captain Hull recorded Montresor's words:

> Hale at once declared his name, his rank in the American army, and his object in coming within the British lines.

Sir William Howe, without the form of a trial, gave orders for his execution the following morning. He was placed in the custody of the provost marshal, who was . . . hardened to human suffering and every softening sentiment of the heart. Captain Hale, alone, without sympathy or support, save that from above, on the near approach of death asked for a clergyman to attend him. It was refused. He then requested a Bible; that too was refused by his inhuman jailer.

On the morning of his execution . . . my station was near the fatal spot, and I requested the provost marshal to permit the prisoner to sit in my marquee, while he was making the necessary preparations. Captain Hale entered: he was calm, and bore himself with gentle dignity, in the consciousness of rectitude and high intentions. He asked for writing materials, which I furnished him: he wrote two letters . . . He was shortly after summoned to the gallows. But a few persons were around him, yet his characteristic dying words were remembered. He said, "I only regret, that I have but one life to lose for my country."

A brief excerpt from a letter written at Coventry, Connecticut, the following spring by Nathan Hale's father, Richard, who had six sons altogether in the Revolution, betrays the deep grief of this unlettered man:

You desired me to inform you about my son Nathan. . . .
He was executed about the twenty-second of September

last by the accounts we have had. A child I sot much by
but he is gone. . . .

This letter, addressed to Richard Hale's brother, Major Samuel
Hale, in Portsmouth, New Hampshire, on March 28, 1777, was
put away in a secret drawer of the major's desk. In 1908, the old
desk was sold at auction as an antique, and three years later the new
owner, the Honorable Frank L. Howe of Barrington, New Hampshire, chanced upon it. Such is the thrill of historical discovery.

Only a Dad
EDGAR GUEST

*We should not forget to sing praises for devoted fathers—espe-
cially our own. This Edgar Guest poem may help us remember that
the only reward a devoted father seeks is his family's flourishing.*

> Only a dad with a tired face,
> Coming home from the daily race,
> Bringing little of gold or fame
> To show how well he has played the game;
> But glad in his heart that his own rejoice
> To see him come and to hear his voice.
>
> Only a dad with a brood of four,

One of ten million men or more
Plodding along in the daily strife,
Bearing the whips and the scorns of life,
With never a whimper of pain or hate,
For the sake of those who at home await.

Only a dad, neither rich nor proud,
Merely one of the surging crowd,
Toiling, striving from day to day,
Facing whatever may come his way,
Silent whenever the harsh condemn,
And bearing it all for the love of them.

Only a dad but he gives his all,
To smooth the way for his children small,
Doing with courage stern and grim
The deeds that his father did for him.
This is the line that for him I pen:
Only a dad, but the best of men.

Penelope's Web

ADAPTED FROM JAMES BALDWIN

Penelope's long wait for her husband's return from the Trojan War is one of our greatest stories of loyalty. The queen's

patience and love make her one of Greek mythology's most
memorable characters. The story comes from Homer's Odyssey.
In this retelling, Odysseus is called by his Latin name, Ulysses.

Of all the heroes who fought against Troy, the wisest and shrewdest was Ulysses, king of Ithaca. Yet, he went unwillingly to war. He longed to stay at home with his wife, Penelope, and their baby boy, Telemachus. But the princes of Greece demanded that he help them, and at last he consented.

"Go, Ulysses," said Penelope, "and I will keep your home and kingdom safe until you return."

"Do your duty, Ulysses," said his old father, Laertes. "Go, and may wise Athena speed your coming back."

And so, bidding farewell to Ithaca and all he held dear, he sailed away to the Trojan War.

Ten long years passed, and then news reached Ithaca that the weary siege of Troy was ended, the city lay in ashes, and the Greek kings were returning to their native lands. One by one, all the heroes reached their homes, but of Ulysses and his companions there came no word. Every day, Penelope and young Telemachus and feeble old Laertes stood by the shore and gazed with aching eyes far over the waves. But no sign of sail or glinting oars could they discern. Months passed by, and then years, and still no word.

"His ships are wrecked, and he lies at the bottom of the sea," sighed old Laertes, and after that he shut himself up in his narrow room and went no more to the shore.

But Penelope still hoped and hoped. "He is not dead," she

said. "And until he comes home, I will hold this fair kingdom for him."

Every day his seat was placed for him at the table. His coat was hung by his chair, his chamber was dusted, and his great bow that hung in the hall was polished.

Ten more years passed with constant watching. Telemachus became a tall, gentle-mannered young man. And throughout all Greece, men began to talk of nothing but Penelope's great nobility and beauty.

"How foolish of her," the Greek princes and chiefs said, "to be forever looking for Ulysses. Everyone knows he is dead. She ought to marry one of us now."

So one after another, the chiefs and princes who were looking for wives sailed to Ithaca, hoping to win Penelope's love. They were haughty and overbearing fellows, glorying in their own importance and wealth. Straight to the palace they went, not waiting for an invitation, for they knew they would be treated as honored guests, whether they were welcome or not.

"Come now, Penelope," they said, "we all know Ulysses is dead. We have come as suitors for your hand, and you dare not turn us away. Choose one of us, and the rest will depart."

But Penelope answered sadly, "Princes and heroes, this cannot be. I am quite sure Ulysses lives, and I must hold his kingdom for him till he returns."

"Return he never will," said the suitors. "Make your choice now."

"Give me a month longer to wait for him," she pleaded. "In

my loom I have a half-finished web of soft linen. I am weaving it for the shroud of our father, Laertes, who is very old and cannot live much longer. If Ulysses fails to return by the time this web is finished, then I will choose, though unwillingly."

The suitors agreed and made themselves at home in the palace. They seized the best of everything. They feasted daily in the great dining hall, wasting much, and helped themselves to all the wine in the cellar. They were rude and uproarious in the once quiet chambers of the palace, and insulting to the people of Ithaca.

Every day Penelope sat at her loom and wove. "See how much I have added to the length of the web?" she would say when evening came. But at night, when the suitors were asleep, she raveled out all the threads she had woven during the day. Thus although she was always at work, the web was never finished.

As the weeks passed, however, the suitors began to grow weary of waiting.

"When will that web be finished?" they impatiently asked.

"I am busy with it every day," Penelope answered, "but it grows very slowly. Such a delicate piece of work cannot be completed so quickly."

But one of the suitors, a man named Agelaus, was not satisfied. That night he crept quietly through the palace and peeped into the weaving room. There he saw Penelope busily unraveling the web by the light of a little lamp, while she whispered to herself the name of Ulysses.

The next morning the secret was known to every one of the unwelcome guests. "Fair queen," they said, "you are very cunning, but we have found you out. That web must be finished before the sun rises again, and then tomorrow you must make your choice. We shall wait no longer."

The following afternoon the unwelcome guests assembled in the great hall. The feast was set, and they ate and drank and sang and shouted as never before. They made such an uproar that the very timbers of the palace shook.

While the turmoil was at its height, Telemachus came in, followed by Eumaeus, his father's oldest and most faithful servant. Together they began to remove all the shields and swords that hung on the walls and rattled from so much commotion.

"What are you doing with those weapons?" shouted the suitors, who finally noticed the old man and the youth.

"They are becoming tarnished with smoke and dust," said Eumaeus, "and will keep much better in the treasure room."

"But we will leave my father's great bow that hangs at the head of the hall," added Telemachus. "My mother polishes it every day, and she would sadly miss it if it were removed."

"She won't be polishing it much longer," the suitors laughed. "Before this day is over, Ithaca will have a new king."

At that moment a strange beggar entered the courtyard. His feet were bare, his head was uncovered, his clothes were in rags. He approached the kitchen door, where an old greyhound, Argos, was lying on a heap of ashes. Twenty years before, Argos had been Ulysses' favorite and most loyal hunting dog. But now, grown toothless and almost blind, he was only abused by the suitors.

When he saw the beggar slowly moving through the yard,

he raised his head to look. Then a strange look came suddenly into his old eyes. His tail wagged feebly, and he tried with all his failing strength to rise. He looked up lovingly into the beggar's face, and uttered a long but joyful howl like that which he once uttered in his youth when greeting his master.

The beggar stooped and patted his head. "Argos, old friend," he whispered.

The dog staggered to his feet, then fell, and was dead with the look of joy still in his eyes.

A moment later the beggar stood in the doorway of the great hall, where he was seen whispering a few words to Telemachus and faithful Eumaeus.

"What do you want here, Old Rags?" the suitors called, hurling crusts of bread at his head. "Get out! Be gone!"

But at that moment, down the stairs came Penelope, stately and beautiful, with her servants and maids around her.

"The queen! The queen!" cried the suitors. "She has come to choose one of us!"

"Telemachus, my son," said Penelope, "what poor man is this whom our guests treat so roughly?"

"Mother, he is a wandering beggar whom the waves cast upon our shores last night," answered the prince. "He says that he brings news of my father."

"Then he shall tell me of it," said the queen. "But first he must rest." At this she caused the beggar to be led to a seat at the farther side of the room, and gave orders that he be fed and refreshed.

An old woman, who had been Ulysses' nurse when he

was a child, brought a great bowl of water and towels. Kneeling on the stones before the stranger, she began to wash his feet. Suddenly she sprang back, overturning the bowl in her confusion.

"O, master! The scar!" she muttered quietly.

"Dear nurse," whispered the beggar, "you were ever discreet and wise. You know me by the old scar I have carried on my knee since boyhood. Keep well the secret, for I bide my time, and the hour of vengeance is nigh."

This man in rags was indeed Ulysses, the king. Alone in a little boat he had been cast, that very morning, upon the shore of his own island. He had made himself known to Telemachus and old Eumaeus alone, and by his orders they had removed the weapons that hung on the wall of the great hall.

Meanwhile, the suitors had gathered again around the feast table and were more boisterous than before. "Come, fair Penelope!" they shouted. "This beggar can tell his tale tomorrow. It is time for you to choose a new husband! Choose now!"

"Chiefs and princes," said Penelope, in trembling tones, "let us leave this decision to the gods. Behold, there hangs the great bow of Ulysses, which he alone was able to string. Let each of you try his strength in bending it, and I will choose the one who can shoot an arrow from it the most skillfully."

"Well said!" cried all the suitors, and they lined up to try their strength. The first took the bow in his hands, and struggled long to bend it. Then, losing patience, he threw it on the ground and strode away. "None but a giant can string a bow like that," he said.

Then, one by one, the other suitors tried their strength, but all in vain.

"Perhaps the old beggar would like to take part in this contest," one said with a sneer.

Then Ulysses in his beggar's rags rose from his seat and went with halting steps to the head of the hall. He fumbled with the great bow, gazing at its polished back and its long, well-shaped arms, stout as bars of iron. "Methinks," he said, "that in my younger days I once saw a bow like this."

"Enough! Enough!" shouted the suitors. "Get out, you old fool!"

Suddenly, a great change came over the stranger. Almost without effort, he bent the great bow and strung it. Then he rose to his full height, and even in his beggar's rags appeared every inch a king.

"Ulysses! Ulysses!" Penelope cried.

The suitors were speechless. Then, in the wildest alarm, they turned and tried to escape from the hall. But the arrows of Ulysses were swift and sure, and not one missed its mark. "Now I avenge myself upon those who have tried to destroy my home!" he cried. And thus, one after another, the lawless suitors perished.

The next day Ulysses sat in the great hall with Penelope and Telemachus and all the joyful members of the household, and he told the story of his long wanderings over the sea. And Penelope, in turn, related how she had faithfully kept the kingdom, as she had promised, though beset by insolent and wicked suitors. Then she brought from her chamber a roll of soft, white cloth of wonderful delicacy and beauty, and said, "This is the web, Ulysses. I promised that on the day of its completion I would choose a husband, and I choose you."

The Story of Cincinnatus

RETOLD BY JAMES BALDWIN

This story takes place in 458 B.C., when Rome was attacked by a tribe called the Aequi. It reminds us that the loyal citizen expects no great reward for coming to his country's aid.

There was a man named Cincinnatus who lived on a little farm not far from the city of Rome. He had once been rich, and had held the highest office in the land, but in one way or another he had lost all his wealth. He was now so poor that he had to do all the work on his farm with his own hands. But in those days it was thought to be a noble thing to till the soil.

Cincinnatus was so wise and just that everybody trusted him, and asked his advice. When anyone was in trouble, and did not know what to do, his neighbors would say,

"Go and tell Cincinnatus. He will help you."

Now there lived among the mountains, not far away, a tribe of fierce, half-wild men, who were at war with the Roman people. They persuaded another tribe of bold warriors to help them, and then marched toward the city, plundering and robbing as they came. They boasted that they would tear down the walls of Rome, and burn the houses, and kill all the men, and make slaves of the women and children.

At first the Romans, who were very proud and brave, did not think there was much danger. Every man in Rome was a soldier, and the army which went out to fight the robbers was the finest in the world. No one stayed at home but the white-haired "Fathers," as they were called, who made the laws for the city, and a small company of men who guarded the walls. Everybody thought that it would be an easy thing to drive the men of the mountains back to the place where they belonged.

But one morning five horsemen came riding down the road from the mountains. They rode with great speed, and both men and horses were covered with dust and blood. The watchman at the gate knew them and shouted to them as they galloped in. Why did they ride thus? And what had happened to the Roman army?

They did not answer him, but rode into the city and along the quiet streets. Everybody ran after them, eager to find out what was the matter. Rome was not a large city at that time, and soon they reached the marketplace where the white-haired Fathers were sitting. Then they leaped from their horses, and told their story.

"Only yesterday," they said, "our army was marching through a narrow valley between two steep mountains. All at once a thousand savage men sprang out from among the rocks before us and above us. They had blocked up the way, and the pass was so narrow that we could not fight. We tried to come back, but they had blocked up the way on this side of us, too. The fierce men of the mountains were before us and behind us, and they were throwing rocks down upon us from above. We had been caught in a trap. Then ten of us set spurs to our horses, and five of us forced our way through, but the other five fell before the spears of the mountain men. And now, O Roman Fathers! Send help to our army at once, or every man will be slain, and our city will be taken."

"What shall we do?" said the white-haired Fathers. "Whom can we send but the guards and the boys? And who is wise enough to lead them and thus save Rome?"

All shook their heads and were very grave, for it seemed as if there was no hope. Then one said, "Send for Cincinnatus. He will help us."

Cincinnatus was in the field plowing when the men who had been sent to him came in great haste. He stopped and greeted them kindly, and waited for them to speak.

"Put on your cloak, Cincinnatus," they said, "and hear the words of the Roman people."

Then Cincinnatus wondered what they could mean. "Is all well with Rome?" he asked. And he called to his wife to bring him his cloak.

She brought the cloak; and Cincinnatus wiped the dust from his hands and arms, and threw it over his shoulder. Then the men told their errand.

They told him how the army with all the noblest men of Rome had been entrapped in the mountain pass. They told him about the great danger the city was in. Then they said, "The people of Rome make you their ruler and the ruler of their city, to do with everything as you choose. And the Fathers bid you come at once and go out against our enemies, the fierce men of the mountains."

So Cincinnatus left his plow standing where it was, and hurried to the city. When he passed through the streets, and gave orders as to what should be done, some of the people were afraid, for they knew that he had all power in Rome to do what he pleased. But he armed the guards and the boys, and went out at their head to fight the fierce mountain men, and free the Roman army from the trap into which it had fallen.

A few days afterward there was great joy in Rome. There was good news from Cincinnatus. The men of the mountains had been beaten with great loss. They had been driven back into their own place.

And now the Roman army, with the boys and the guards, was coming home with banners flying, and shouts of victory. And at their head rode Cincinnatus. He had saved Rome.

Cincinnatus might then have made himself king, for his word was law, and no man dared lift a finger against him. But, before the people could thank him enough for what he had done, he gave back the power to the white-haired Roman Fathers, and went again to his little farm and his plow.

He had been the ruler of Rome for sixteen days.

Thunder Falls

RETOLD BY ALLAN MACFARLAN

This story comes from the Kickapoo Indians, a Midwestern tribe once noted for their frequent wanderings; their name comes from a word meaning "he who moves about, standing now here, now there."

The blanket of night had wrapped the Kickapoo village in darkness. The people were gathered around the story-fire, awaiting the tale which the storyteller would tell. The listeners knew that the tale would not be of braves on the war trail or warriors who risked their lives on raids into the country of their enemies. And yet the story which they were about to hear was one of high courage. It was of two brave women who were still honored in song and dance because of their great courage and their noble sacrifice made for their tribe. This is the story that the people heard.

A band of our men were hunting, when the green earth had come from beneath the snow and rivers were fat and fast. Women were with the men, to help skin the animals taken in the chase, and to strip and dry the meat. For three suns the party had hunted, and deer had fallen to their hunting arrows.

As they traveled in country distant from our territory, there was always danger of attack by enemies. Braves kept watch always, but they did not watch well enough. One day the chief said it would be a good thing to return to the tribe, and the party made ready to go back when the sun came. Some of the braves and women did not see the sun again. A big war party of Shawnee surrounded and attacked the camp when night was leaving to let morning come.

The Kickapoo who were not killed or badly wounded escaped down into the gorges. They had hunted there and found a great cave, beneath the thundering falls of a mighty river. The chief had decided that they would hide there if they saw a large war party of the enemy, so all of the Kickapoo knew the hiding place.

The savage Shawnee killed the wounded and took two of our

women back to their camp, as prisoners. The women were young and would be made to work. The camp of the Shawnee was far above the place where they had attacked our party. Their lodges were on the banks of the wide, fast-flowing river.

For six suns after the attack, the Shawnee warriors searched for our people who had escaped the raid. Sentries were placed at distant points so that the Kickapoo could not escape without being seen. The big war party of the Shawnee would be told of their movements. The enemy searched well, but our people hid better and were not discovered. Our chief did not let his party leave the great cavern, nor did they need to, for they had dried meat and water in plenty.

After some suns had passed, the people begged the chief to let them leave the shelter of the big cave beneath the falls. They felt safe there, but the terrible noise of the falls hurt their ears, as it roared like a curtain of thunder before the cavern. Their minds were afraid too, for they feared that spirits of evil dwelt in the dark, rocky gorges which surrounded them.

The chief was brave, but he knew how his band felt. He too would be happy to leave the great roaring and rumbling far behind him, even if, in escaping, more of his band would fall to the arrows of the Shawnee. "Tomorrow, the day of the seventh sun since the attack, will be the last that we remain here," he told his band. "When darkness comes, we will try to escape from the enemy into our own territory. Be ready!"

Our chief knew that the chances of reaching safety were few, as the Shawnee were many and must be angry that any of our people had escaped the raid. "Their anger must be very great," the

Kickapoo chief thought, "because though they could follow the trails in the forest, their best trailers could not see footprints on the rocky ground which formed the river gorges."

The medicine man of the Shawnee went to their chief on the morning of the seventh sun and told him of a dream which he had had. His totem bird, the red-tailed hawk, had come to him in a dream and flown around and around him in circles, giving shrill cries and tempting him to follow it. The medicine man could not refuse to follow his totem bird, so his spirit followed it as it flew swiftly before him, until the hawk reached a clearing in the forest. Here, in the dream, the medicine man saw a circle of Shadow People.

"Can I follow the Shadow People to where our enemies are hidden?" the medicine man asked the hawk. "Who among them knows where the band is hiding?"

The hawk flew straight to the two women who were the prisoners of the Shawnee and circled the head of each.

"These women must know," declared the medicine man, as he told his chief of the dream. "My hawk totem never leads me on a false trail."

The Shawnee chief had great faith in the medicine man and his totem bird; so he called a council of his warriors. He told them of the dream and had the two captive women brought before him. When questioned, they declared that they did not know where the band to which they belonged was hidden.

"They speak with a crooked tongue," shouted the medicine man, "but torture will make it straight."

The women were tortured and, under the bite of blazing

twigs held to their wrists, they cried out that they would reveal the hiding place of their band. For a moment, they spoke softly together in their own dialect and then, by signs, showed that they were ready to lead the Shawnee war party to the hiding place.

When the Shawnee were armed and about to follow them, the two women pointed to the river, instead of leading the way into the forest. By signs they showed that our people were far away and could be reached quicker by the Shawnees if they went by canoe. When the chief pointed toward the forest and his braves pushed the women in that direction, they showed by sign talk that they could not lead the Shawnees by land. Only by water did they know the way to the hidden Kickapoo band.

The chief believed the women, and they were taken to the big canoes that lay on the riverbank. With hands and sounds, the women told that close to the falls there was a little branch of the main river which they must follow to reach the Kickapoo. The chief ordered the women into the leading canoe. He too sat in it, with his medicine man and six of his best warriors. The rest of the party followed close behind, in many canoes. Paddles flashed and the canoes went swift as a fish downstream.

After paddling far, the chief asked the women if they were not yet near the hiding place of his enemies. The women sign-talked that the place was near, and again the paddles rose and fell. The braves did not have to paddle so hard now because the current was becoming swifter and stronger, as the canoes sped along. Quicker and quicker the canoes traveled. From the distance came the thunder of the falls. Closer and closer came the earth-shaking roar.

The chief was brave, but even he feared the mighty force of the swift-rushing waters. He was directly behind the two captive women, who sat in the bow. He touched them on the shoulders, and they turned to him at once. The chief ceased to fear when he saw that both women were smiling. The elder of the two, with a wave of her arm toward the south bank, showed that in a moment they would reach the fork of the river, where the paddlers could swing the canoes from the rushing current into the calm water of the smaller stream.

Faster, ever faster, the canoes now dashed through the foaming torrent. Narrower grew the rushing river as it roared between solid walls of rock. No time to try to turn the canoes!

Too late, the chief and warriors knew that they had been tricked. The bravest had but time to sing a few notes of their death songs before the raging torrent swept the shattered canoes over the crest of the mighty waterfall. Proudly leading the band of enemy warriors to death on the jagged rocks below were the two brave women of the Kickapoo.

My story is done, but that of the two who saved our band of warriors from death will go on as long as grass grows and water runs.

Yudisthira at Heaven's Gate

This story is from the Mahabharata, *which, with the* Ramayana, *is one of the two great epic poems of India. Here loyalty is literally the test to gain entrance to heaven.*

Good King Yudisthira had ruled over the Pandava people for many years and had led them in a successful, but very long war against giant forces of evil. At the end of his labors, Yudisthira felt that he had had enough years on earth and it was time to go on to the kingdom of the Immortals. When all his plans were made, he set out for the high Mount Meru to go from there to the Celestial City. His beautiful wife, Drapaudi, went with him and also his four brothers. Very soon, they were joined by a dog which followed quietly behind him.

But the journey to the mountain was a long and sorrowful one. Yudisthira's four brothers died one by one along the way, and after that his wife, the beautiful Drapaudi. The King was all alone then, except for the dog, which continued to follow him faithfully up and up the steep, long road to the Celestial City.

At last the two, weak and exhausted, stopped before the gates of Heaven. Yudisthira bowed humbly there as he asked to be admitted.

Sky and earth were filled with a loud noise as the God Indra, God of a Thousand Eyes, arrived to meet and welcome the King to Paradise. But Yudisthira was not quite ready.

"Without my brothers and my beloved wife, my innocent Drapaudi, I do not wish to enter Heaven, O Lord of all the deities," he said.

"Have no fear," Indra answered. "You shall meet them all in Heaven. They came before you and are already there!"

But Yudisthira had yet another request to make.

"This dog has come all the way with me. He is devoted to me.

Surely for his faithfulness I cannot leave him outside! And besides, my heart is full of love for him!"

Indra shook his great head and the earth quaked.

"You yourself may have immortality," he said, "and riches and success and all the joys of Heaven. You have won these by making this hard journey. But you cannot bring a dog into Heaven. Cast off the dog, Yudisthira! It is no sin!"

"But where would he go?" demanded the King. "And who would go with him? He has given up all the pleasures of earth to be my companion. I cannot desert him now."

The God was irritated at this.

"You must be pure to enter Paradise," he said firmly. "Just to touch a dog will take away all the merits of prayer. Consider what you are doing, Yudisthira. Let the dog go!"

But Yudisthira insisted. "O God of a Thousand Eyes, it is difficult for a person who has always tried to be righteous to do something that he knows is unrighteous—even in order to get into Heaven. I do not wish immortality if it means casting off one that is devoted to me."

Indra urged him once more.

"You left on the road behind you your four brothers and your wife. Why can't you also leave the dog?"

But Yudisthira said, "I abandoned those only because they had died already and I could no longer help them nor bring them back to life. As long as they lived I did not leave them."

"You are willing to abandon Heaven, then, for this dog's sake?" the God asked him.

"Great God of all Gods," Yudisthira replied, "I have steadily kept this vow—that I will never desert one that is frightened and seeks my protection, one that is afflicted and destitute, or one that is too weak to protect himself and desires to live. Now I add a fourth. I have promised never to forsake one that is devoted to me. I will not abandon my friend."

Yudisthira reached down to touch the dog and was about to turn sadly away from Heaven when suddenly before his very eyes a wonder happened. The faithful dog was changed into Dharma, the God of Righteousness and Justice.

Indra said, "You are a good man, King Yudisthira. You have shown faithfulness to the faithful, and compassion for all creatures. You have done this by renouncing the very Gods themselves instead of renouncing this humble dog that was your companion. You shall be honored in heaven, O King Yudisthira, for there is no act which is valued more highly and rewarded more richly than compassion for the humble."

So Yudisthira entered the Celestial City with the God of Righteousness beside him. He was reunited there with his brothers and his beloved wife to enjoy eternal happiness.

Afterword

Life is full of questions, and most of us spend much of our time thinking about the relatively unimportant ones. What time does the game come on TV? Do these shoes go with these pants? Will I get that new bike for my birthday? These are the questions of daily living, and they are natural enough. There is nothing wrong with them. But we need to spend some time thinking about the truly important questions, too, the ones that lead to *better* living. This book will help you find answers to three of them: What are virtues? Why do you need them? How do you get them?

The dictionary defines *virtue* as "a particular moral excellence" and tells us it comes from the Latin word virtus, meaning "strength" or "worth." Virtues come in several different varieties, and this book focuses on five of them—friendship, work, courage, honesty, and loyalty. The stories, poems, and writings in this book will help you recognize these character traits, both in yourself and in others, in part by showing you examples of virtues in action. (Remember, virtues for the most part lie in our actions—good deeds, not just good thoughts and intentions.) The more you witness virtues in action, the better you'll understand them. You need very clear understandings of virtues if you are to get them. And you need equally clear understandings of vices, and their consequences, if you are to steer clear of them.

Why do you need virtues? You'll meet several answers to that question in these pages. There are practical reasons: Your reputation, for example, is largely the sum of your virtues. There are social reasons: The kind and number of friends you have will depend on your own virtues. And there are, of course, purely unselfish reasons: Virtues are the character traits that move us to help family, loved ones, and even perfect strangers. In every area of life, you must constantly make choices about how to act, for your own sake and for others'. Many of those choices involve matters of right and wrong, and you can't choose to do the right thing without possessing some virtues.

So how do you get (and keep) these virtues? The answer is one of those solutions that is easier said than done. You practice. Like anything else worthwhile, attaining virtue requires serious effort and attention. You must set some standards for yourself and then do everything you can to live up to them in your *everyday activities*. Hopefully, you will find models and standards in the stories and other writings in this book. People have been using some of them for centuries as reminders of what is good and what is bad, as moral compasses to right and wrong. If you take these stories to heart and pattern your own actions after the examples they set, you'll begin to find that these notions of honesty and loyalty and self-discipline are becoming habits. That's what you want. That's what we all want. When the virtues are a matter of habit for you, you're well equipped to face life. Remember too that none of us can be virtuous all the time. We are not angels, and we can't become angels, at least not in this life. But we can try to be better, and so we should.

—William J. Bennett

About the Authors

WILLIAM J. BENNETT is host of the top-ten nationally syndicated radio show *Bill Bennett's Morning in America* and is the Washington Fellow of the Claremont Institute. He served as secretary of education and chairman of the National Endowment for the Humanities under President Reagan, and as director of the Office of National Drug Control Policy under President George H. W. Bush. Dr. Bennett and his wife, Elayne, live in Chevy Chase, Maryland.

DOUG FLUTIE is a fan-favorite quarterback who played professionally for twenty-one years. In his senior year at Boston College, Doug won the Heisman Trophy and All American and Player of the Year honors. Over his pro career, Doug threw for 58,150 yards, ranking third in football history. In 1998, in honor of their son, Doug and his wife, Laurie, began the nationally renowned Doug Flutie, Jr. Foundation for Autism.